Made in the USA
Columbia, SC
07 November 2017

Dedication

For Noelene
who helps me wise up

Books by William G. Johnsson

Behold His Glory
Blessed Assurance
Clean!
The Great Physician
Hebrews
In Absolute Confidence
Religion in Overalls
Why Doesn't Anyone Care?
Why I Am a Seventh-day Adventist

**Books by William G. Johnsson
and Noelene Johnsson**

I Chose Adventism
The Wit and Wisdom of Charles Bradford

Contents

Preface

This is a fun book, written for enjoyment, for me and my friends. It's a child of *Behold His Glory*. That collection of devotional reflections brought more letters, telephone calls, and greetings from strangers than everything else combined that I ever wrote.

Over and over people said they liked best the personal side of the book. The things big or little (they were mainly little) that I shared and talked about from a Christian approach to life.

So this child is directly and deliberately personal. But I hope it's much more: Just talking about myself and my family and my friends would be an ego trip—and a bore. I hope that this collection of bits of life, not arranged to prove a point or to develop a pattern, will point to a Pattern.

For this I believe:

1. There is a God, infinitely great, infinitely wise, infinitely loving.

2. God knows us, and we can know Him.

3. Jesus Christ has made God known.

4. The essence of all that counts in this life and the hereafter is love.

5. A good and faithful wife or husband is an inestimable gift.

6. Kids are worth all the pain, expense, and trauma.

7. To be loyal to friends counts more than winning the world.

8. Life is interesting; life is good.

9. Life in Jesus Christ is the best there is—now and forever.

10. Beauty and goodness are only a glance away.

Things little or big, things funny or dumb, things amazing or ordinary—they make up a life, and they make up this book.

Did Malachi have them in mind when he wrote: "Then those who feared the Lord talked with each other, and the Lord listened and heard. A scroll of remembrance was written in his presence concerning those who feared the Lord and honored his name. 'They will be mine,' says the Lord Almighty, 'in the day when I make up my treasured possession'" (Mal. 3:16, 17, NIV)?

CHAPTER 1

Wising Up

You can break down my life in various ways. One of the most revealing would be in terms of life before and after I wised up. Before I wised up (BIWU), I was a shocking chauvinist. Well, maybe you could find one or two redeeming qualities. If I wasn't quite a male chauvinist pig, I was an M. C. piglet.

Remember, I grew up in Australia. The Great South Land was a *man's* country. It still is. About the most endearing term of the culture is "mate." But the Oz's use of "mate" has nothing to do with what birds and rabbits do. It's along the lines of "buddy" or "pal." And here's the catch: Mateship belongs exclusively to males down under. A man's mate is his close friend—and a woman doesn't rate. (She's a "sheila" if single, the "missus" if his wife.)

For generations the sacred place of mateship was the bar. A males-only domain. I didn't grow up with bars, but I grew up in the world of mateship. Without anyone telling me how the world fit together or how it might be different, I grew up a shocking chauvinist. In fact, that word wasn't part of people's vocabulary, let alone their thinking.

At Avondale College I met Noelene and we fell in love.

Noelene was different. She had a good mind, and it was all her own. She wasn't afraid to express it—even though males had a hard time recognizing its quality. (In group conversations, the men would pick up where the previous man had left off, as though Noelene—or any woman, for that matter—hadn't spoken.)

I wasn't put off by Noelene's breaking the woman's code of silence. Her father, however, a good Adventist minister, found her opinions difficult to swallow. Her three brothers were a bit more accepting. But they—and I also—retained our shocking chauvinism. It was still a man's country and a man's world.

Well, we married and left Australia for 15 years in India. I didn't wise up right away, but some things began to change.

In India I began to realize that I harbored racist feelings. That was something I could not have accepted about myself earlier. If you had suggested it to me back in Australia, I would have laughed and pointed out that one of my best friends was Ethiopian. Although he was very black, he ate at our table and slept under our roof the summer we sold books together.

But racist feelings are selective. I didn't harbor racist feelings toward Black people per se or toward Indians. But the Aborigines of Australia—I grew up regarding them as more than animals but less than human. I don't recall anyone ever telling me that. I don't think any teacher taught us that. But the Oz culture held those attitudes, and I sucked them up.

It's good to be wrenched out of your culture, to stand alone in an alien land. You begin to see yourself and your native country in new light. I remember attending a public meeting to hear Pandit Jawaharlal Nehru, prime minister of India. Another White man and I sat right in front of him, and we were the only foreigners in a crowd of perhaps 20,000. At one point Nehru, who had been speaking in Hindi, stopped, looked straight at us, and broke into English. After a while he reverted to Hindi.

Experiences like that had their effect. Slowly, over the years, I began to wise up. I don't remember any moment of truth, any revelation about my racism. But eventually I saw myself in a new way, a way that separated me from my family members and friends back in Oz.

I was wising up. I was able to recognize my racist attitudes. And to be ashamed of them. I still had a long way to go. I was still a shocking chauvinist.

After our two children started school, Noelene went back to school. She completed her baccalaureate degree when we lived at Spicer College, and later her M.A. when we moved to Andrews University.

Then in 1980 the General Conference called us to Washington, D.C. I began work at the *Adventist Review;* Noelene edited the mission quarterlies.

By now our life together had changed quite a bit. We both worked full-time. And slowly, slowly, I began to realize that the home chores—the vacuuming, the cleaning, the laundry, the shopping, the meals—ought to be shared. We both were glad for the paycheck Noelene brought home, but it simply wasn't fair to expect her to do everything at home also.

I was starting to wise up.

But it was tough. For a while I resented even giving a little help—I was a grudging participant. But eventually the Lord—and Noelene—got through to me, and I saw the light.

A major change for me came in 1985. Prior to that, Noelene had put together the senior and junior editions of *Mission*, based on materials sent in from the overseas fields. But after the General Conference session that year, Southern Asia asked her to come in person, gather the materials, and write the stories herself.

She went—for a couple weeks. And I was left. We had been married 25 years, and always *I* had done the traveling. Now I learned what it is like to be left at home while your spouse goes away on a work assignment. Married 25 years, and I didn't know how to run the dishwasher. Married 25 years, and I didn't know how to operate the clothes washer and dryer.

(I kid you not. This is all true. Now you'll more readily agree with my self-description as a shocking chauvinist.)

Before she left, Noelene explained everything. She pasted little yellow stickers on the appliances: "Turn to 14, and press the button."

I didn't want to learn. This was her world. But the dishes stacked up in the dishwasher, and the clothes began to run low. I began to experiment with these gadgets from her world, and—voila!—I got them to work.

That trip to India proved to be the first of several overseas assignments for her. She went on her own to Africa—not to a comfortable station like Nairobi, but to Rwanda and Madagascar. Then South America invited her. And Inter-America. And Euro-Africa. And the Far East. Then Southern Asia again. All these trips of a couple week's duration were on her own.

They weren't easy for her. Or for me.

During these years I traveled a lot also. We missed each other. We relished the trips—few though they were—when we could travel together.

Years of adjustment, years of growth. Our relationship was tested. It flexed, bent to accommodate the changes. We were still in love, but with new appreciation and understanding. We were truly equals—adults, mature servants of the Lord, each with a calling and a ministry. We were pulling together for the same goal. Only now Noelene wasn't merely supporting me in my ministry. She was fulfilling her own calling and ministry.

For a while I loved what she was doing and hated it. But the Lord kept working on me. Now I'm proud of her and her work.

And I have wised up. I'm no longer a shocking chauvinist.

CHAPTER 2

News Freak

L ong before I got into editorial work, as far back as I can remember, I have been interested in news and newspapers. I'm not quite ready to kill to get the news, but don't press it.

One August morning, before setting out for school, I scanned the pages of the *Advertiser*, the daily for my hometown of Adelaide in southern Australia. Over on the left, toward the bottom of the front page, the paper carried in red type late news—"Stop Press." This morning the box briefly reported on a new type of bomb—far more powerful than anything before invented—that had been dropped on Japan.

That afternoon on my way home I saw copies of the evening paper, the *News*. In huge black letters it announced the atomic bomb. We didn't take the evening paper, so after I reached home I got on my bicycle and set out to buy one. But every store had sold out. I pedaled on and on, stopping every time I saw a *News* sign, inquiring for miles, until I found a newsstand that still had a copy. I took home my copy of the *News* and read about the annihilation of Hiroshima.

Once Noelene and I spent a month at the Adventist college in France. Nestled under the brow of a great cliff, the Saleve, it overlooks Geneva. Hang gliders leap off the Saleve and float down for miles, landing in Switzerland.

It's a place of spectacular beauty. And isolated.

We didn't have a car.

Geneva was miles away below us.

And we had no radio or television. Even if we had, our French was minimal.

How did we get the news? We went—make that walked—to Geneva.

Well, sometimes we got a ride down to the Swiss border. But we always *walked* back—and the grade is steep.

At the border we caught a bus that took us several miles to the end of the trolley line. Then we hopped onto a trolley for Geneva.

And in Geneva? The *Herald Tribune!* Sometimes a cone with Italian *gelato* (and the scoop is really small). But the *Herald Tribune* was what we came for.

We'd stand on the bridge over the river, watching the swift, cold waters rushing into Lake Geneva. We'd sit on a bench and try to make the cone stretch out. And we'd peek into our treasure.

Then over to the trolley, then to the bus, past French immigration, and up the long hill.

Except for the stock market listings, I read every word in some of those copies of the *Herald Tribune*.

These days we live in Silver Spring, Maryland. One of the great compensations of this high-cost area is waking up to the Washington *Post* on the doorstep.

You can write me down as an incurable news freak.

Maybe that's why I love the Bible. It's full of news, and—unlike our newspapers—most of it is good.

The Greeks had a word for news—*euaggelion*. Long before Christians came on the scene, the Greeks associated *euaggelion* with a messenger who brought a good report.

In fact, *euaggelion* was a technical term for news of victory. The messenger would appear, lift his right arm in greeting, and call out in a loud voice: "Rejoice, we won!" The messenger's very appearance signaled that he brought good news: his face shone, he wore a crown on his head, he swung a branch of palms, his spear was decked with laurel.

At this message the city would go wild. The people would garland the temples and offer sacrifices of thanksgiving. And they would honor the messenger with a wreath.

Then Jesus of Nazareth appeared. Profoundly impacted by His life, teachings, and death—especially the death, because of what His followers believed happened that Sunday morning—Christians looked for a word that said it best. They plucked out the centuries-old term *euangelion*, but filled it with new content.

That is the word we translate "gospel."

I'm an incurable news freak. But even more I'm an incurable gospel—good news—freak.

CHAPTER 3

Tribute

In my BIWU days, I was a reluctant shopper. No, make that rebellious. I hated to shop. The racks and racks of suits rattled me. The shop assistants rattled me. The crowds rattled me.

Waste of time, I rationalized. Why spend hours comparing prices? My argument was: Time is money, so buy the first thing that fits and looks OK, and hightail it out of there.

You guessed it—Noelene loves to shop. She enjoys going to the supermarket, enjoys even more the malls.

So for quite a few years our marital bliss was punctured by Memorial Days at the mall and sales days and supermarkets. I would look at my watch, fume, pout, and whine—and sweat over the KO to our Visa and MasterCard.

Then I wised up. And part of the wising up meant doing the grocery shopping. The issue was quite simple, really: the house had to be vacuumed, and we had to eat.

I hated shopping, but I hated vacuuming even more. So I started doing the shopping, while Noelene did the vacuuming. Which in turn led to a few changes—in the form of additions—to the grocery list Noelene wrote out for me.

Sometime during those early wising up days, I began to bring home flowers with the weekend shopping. And I have never stopped. Noelene has not once put flowers on the list, but for years now my Thursday night or Friday afternoon safari to Giant Food has not once failed to bag a bunch of flowers.

Carnations. Red ones. Five. With one or two pieces of fern. Plus one of those little packs of flower food that make the blooms happy.

Sometimes the store has sold out of carnations, or the ones they have will be black on the edges—a sure sign they will shrivel up within a day or two at home. (I've become an expert on red carnations.) Then I settle for one of those bunches of mixed flowers, occasionally for a mum or gloxinia in a pot.

But carnations—five red ones—are what I go for. I bring them home triumphantly. They are the badge of my male liberation since I have wised up.

Ever bought flowers at a supermarket? Notice how the people in line and the checkers react.

Women, whether customers or checkers, look impressed and cluck a little at how pretty they are.

Male customers look at the flowers, look at you, and don't say a word.

The male checkers are a different story. "You must be in trouble!" I got one night, with a sympathetic look.

Another said: "Who's the lucky girl? You got a big night tonight?"

"Actually, they're for my wife," I told him quietly.

"No way. Don't give me that!" And he shook his head.

But they were.

And they are.

Just now, in the corner by the kitchen sink, you'll find five red carnations in a vase. Two pieces of fern. They're lasting well. Last Friday afternoon I brought them home, clipped the stems, and added that miracle powder to the water. Noelene normally takes care of the flowers, but she's away—in Portland, Oregon, for meetings.

Those carnations are a tribute—my tribute to the woman I love. And who helped me wise up.

Yesterday I spoke at a meeting myself. When it was over, the organizer said, "Thanks, great job. And you looked fantastic. Tell Noelene she's doing it right!"

I didn't tell her. I bought that outfit myself, on my own. And it took me three trips to the mall to get it right.

CHAPTER 4

What I *Didn't* Learn in Kindergarten

Robert Fulghum's *All I Really Need to Know I Learned in Kindergarten* is delightful. And also incomplete. Some things I really needed to know I *didn't* learn in kindergarten. In fact, I didn't learn them in elementary school, or high school, or college. Not even in graduate school.

Wising up came later. And I hope I haven't finished yet. When I stop wising up I'll be ready to be deep-sixed.

So here's my list of life beyond kindergarten:

1. I won't die if I miss a meal.
2. I won't collapse if I don't get a good night's sleep.
3. It's more important to be reliable than brilliant.
4. "If only . . . ," "I should have . . . ," and "I wish I had . . . " are useless expressions and useless for living.
5. I can change.
6. Don't put the blame on Mame, or Mom, or anyone. Take charge, and take the responsibility.
7. Everything good or great or worthwhile is simple at heart.

Kids think they'll die if they miss a meal. They keep count of the number of pieces of pie on the table and try to size up which is the largest. To miss out on a meal because they've been naughty or whatever means they'll surely drop dead.

But they won't. And we won't either. In fact, we may feel better and be better for it. The body can miss a lot of meals—a string of them—and keep going. Jesus didn't eat for 40 days.

I'm not an ascetic. I enjoy eating. But eating isn't the end all of existence.

Nor is sleeping. I used to think that if I didn't get my regular seven to eight hours, I could expect to have a terrible day. That was warrant for being mean: "The baby kept me awake all night . . . I didn't sleep a wink . . . I'm really tired today." Blah, blah, blah. Excuses, excuses, excuses.

After I wised up, I discovered that some of my best days came after a bad night. I may have looked like Dracula, but the sense of sheer need cast me onto the grace of the Lord. And He always comes through. His strength is perfected in our weakness.

So Paul's experience became mine: "But he said to me, 'My grace is sufficient for you, for my power is made perfect in weakness.' Therefore I will boast all the more gladly about my weaknesses, so that Christ's power may rest on me" (2 Cor. 12:9, NIV).

And when it comes to the crunch, any day I'll take an average person who is reliable over a brilliant one who isn't. How many guys with IQs in the 140s are walking around useless, sponging off society? They never finished college, never stuck at anything to make a difference in the world. Because they found out early that grades were a snap and because they could ace a test without cramming, they never learned to push themselves, never learned the value of sticking with a job till it's finished. So they never graduated from the school of life.

A lot of people waste their emotional powers in weasel thinking. OK, so you blew it. What's the value in standing around, wringing your hands, and lamenting about what you *should* have done, or *if* only you hadn't done, or you *wish* you had done?

Get up, get off your duff, and get going.

Kids try to wish away bad things. They play mind games with themselves—to avoid facing up to consequences. I discovered that years ago when I was dean of boys. We had boys 8-18 in that hostel.

There's a fight.

"He hit me!" (Tears, anger, chagrin.)

"Did you hit him?"

"No." (So innocent. How could those blue eyes lie?)

"But you did!" (More tears, etc., plus accusatory tone now.)

"He hit me with a stick!" (Strong accusatory tone.)

Then the big discovery: "I didn't hit him. The *stick* hit him!"

And all this "should" have and "if" and wishing is a throwback to kids' behavior. Time to get beyond the kindergarten.

Because we *can* change. No matter how old or how young, we can change.

We can graduate from kindergarten. At 25 or 35 or 45 or 55 or even 65, we can slough off kindergarten behavior that we have practiced all our life.

We can become a better person.

We can become a nicer person.

We can become a more loving person.

We can become a more beautiful person.

Our God is a God of the new, of change: "Because of the Lord's great love we are not consumed, for his compassions never fail. They are new every morning; great is your faithfulness" (Lam. 3:22, 23, NIV). "Behold, I make all things new" (Rev. 21:5).

For a generation psychologists have been teaching us to blame our mothers—those evil creatures who made us into heaps of inhibitions and bundles of neuroses! Or our alcoholic fathers. Or someone else.

Now, I don't deny the power of our past and the resonance of our roots. We never fully break with our family no matter how hard we try. But we can come to terms with Mother—and with Father and whomever. We can sort out the good from the less good, and be at peace with the past.

And take charge of our lives. Take the responsibility. Bear the blame for what we do *from here on out.*

Life is infinitely complex.

So are we.

But peel away the onion layers, and you'll find the core is simple. Every great person I have met had a basic simplicity. You might have to fight with the peons to get to him or her—the little people who parade their authority and bask in the reflected glory of the one at the top—but it was easy once you got there. Great people live by a few basic principles. In the midst of complex decisions they have a gyroscope that keeps them on course.

Everything great or good or worthwhile in this life is simple at heart. You don't have to be ultrasmart or learned to find that out, but it might take you a long time, a lifetime, to wise up.

Kids could tell us that.
Yes, kids in kindergarten.
If they knew it.

CHAPTER 5

Giant

Scene: a rainy night in Washington, D.C. Groceries in one arm, umbrella in the other, a woman walks along a deserted street.

Suddenly, there's a man. He grabs her purse, punches her in the face, flees.

What does she do? She drops her groceries and runs after him, screaming, "Drop my purse, just drop it!" She chases him three blocks.

They reach Independence Avenue. A man on foot and a woman in a van take up the pursuit. The thief suddenly drops the purse and disappears.

Meet Linda Anne Landers, 26. Giant.

Linda doesn't think of herself as brave. Often at night she'll take a cab for two blocks rather than walk. But when she was attacked at 8:30 p.m. on her way home from the grocery store, she turned into a giant. The blow to her face got something going inside her, and she decided to fight back.

Said Linda: "You never know until you're the victim

of a crime what you're actually capable of."

And every one of us has within possibilities for courage, potential for greatness. We can go beyond our run-of-the-mill selves, think new thoughts, dream and dare and do, and amaze others—and ourselves.

Inside every one of us is a giant ready to take on the world.

The Bible is a book about giants. "The people that do know their God shall be strong, and do exploits," says the book of Daniel (11:32). The book of Hebrews lists some of them and concludes: "And what more shall I say? I do not have time to tell about Gideon, Barak, Samson, Jephthah, David, Samuel and the prophets, who through faith conquered kingdoms, administered justice, and gained what was promised; who shut the mouths of lions, quenched the fury of the flames, and escaped the edge of the sword; whose weakness was turned to strength; and who became powerful in battle and routed foreign armies. Women received back their dead, raised to life again. Others were tortured and refused to be released, so that they might gain a better resurrection. Some faced jeers and flogging, while still others were chained and put in prison. They were stoned; they were sawed in two; they were put to death by the sword. They went about in sheepskins and goatskins, destitute, persecuted and mistreated—the world was not worthy of them. They wandered in deserts and mountains, and in caves and holes in the ground" (Heb. 11:32-38, NIV).

Giants.

I don't know whether Linda Landers is a Christian. The Washington *Post* report of her refusal to be victimized didn't give a clue to her faith. But she's a giant.

And by the way, Linda is four feet eleven inches and weighs 95 pounds.

Giants come in all sizes.

CHAPTER 6

Builders

O n an early-morning walk last Sabbath, I came upon a little old lady pounding on her mailbox. "What's the problem?" I inquired.

"Just look what they did last night," she replied. "I'm afraid it will never be the same again."

Someone had dealt her mailbox a near-lethal blow. One side was stove in, and the lid wouldn't close.

"I think I can fix my box," she went on, "but my neighbors' are worse off."

I looked up the street and had to agree. Mailboxes tilted at drunken angles, sides crumpled, facing away from the curb, lids hanging dejectedly.

And I felt angry.

I realize that this sort of thing happens frequently— often on Friday nights. I'm all for people—young and old—enjoying themselves, but wanton destruction disgusts me.

Some people get their thrills by watching demolition derbies. Others pay good money to see men with sledgehammers destroy cars or furniture. And movie scenes that portray hundreds of dishes being smashed and food flying everywhere are good for belly laughs.

But I don't find destruction funny or entertaining. Any fool with muscles strong enough can destroy. It takes skill and patience to build. I wonder whether those young people—and older ones—who get their kicks out of knocking down mailboxes have ever built anything. I have a hunch that those who have created something with their own hands will be less likely to find pleasure in destroying.

When someone takes a hammer to Michelangelo's *Pieta*, he is arrested. Chances are he'll be placed in a mental home rather than a jail. And we assent to the arrest and the confinement: to destroy a priceless work of art is madness.

We were made in God's image. Although sin has defaced and well-nigh obliterated the image, traces remain. So we humans are godlike in our powers to think and to create. We can dream dreams, think thoughts never before expressed, visualize grand conceptions, and create. Out of the remnant of God's image spring the heavenly melodies of Mozart, the genius of Leonardo da Vinci, the universal vision of Einstein.

We build. We make. We create. We bring form out of the formless, order out of chaos.

All this, I believe, pleases God, who made us like Himself.

That's why destructiveness appalls me. It points back toward madness and darkness; it belongs to the prince of darkness.

But what's all this have to do with Seventh-day Adventists? I doubt that many of us delight in bashing old ladies' mailboxes. Yet, truth is, we are all builders or smashers—and some things are more important than mailboxes.

People, for instance.

And the church.

One of our leaders whom I regard highly has, over the course of a long ministry, shown a consistent concern for the underdog. When a fellow worker fell from grace—because of a mistake or misunderstanding—and others were ready to trample him in the dust, this leader would go to bat for him. At times he placed his own reputation on the line as he sought to reinstate a brother fallen by the way.

Those whom he helped restore to favor have gone on to notable service for the Lord. I know of none who has disappointed the trust placed in him.

And that sort of building is most of all Godlike.

CHAPTER 7

Fathers and Mrs. Fields

The other day I changed planes in Chicago. Strolled around the new United terminal at O'Hare, and chanced upon a Mrs. Fields Cookies store. Admired the selection. Succumbed to the chocolate chip made with milk chocolate.

Just one cookie, in its own bag. Not cheap. But very good.

Ah, Debbi Fields . . .

Debbi grew up in a family with four older sisters. She was the little one, the one left out in games. She was the dumb one, the pest. Early on she learned that her dad badly wanted a son. The doctor told his wife that she oughtn't to have any more children, but that son! So they tried one more time and got—Debbi.

So Debbi tried to be the boy Dad wanted. She'd fly down the street on her bike, scaring the wits out of her mother.

Always Debbi waited to hear magic words. Words that told her she was special, that she could be something in life. But she never heard them—not from Mom, not from Dad, not from Big Sisters.

They sent her off to school. Although her folks weren't good Catholics, they turned Debbi over to the nuns—they could have a turn at being made crazy. Debbi didn't learn much. She spent a lot of time dreaming about how one day she would do something great.

Down in the basement of the home lay an old outboard motor. Her dad, she found out, hoped that one day he'd get enough money to buy a boat for it. And that gave Debbi an idea: one day she'd become wealthy and buy him the boat. Then, at last, her parents would know she really was something special.

In Debbi's senior year of high school, she was chosen homecoming queen. Tingling with excitement, she rushed home to tell the family. As soon as she reached the door, she yelled it out: "I won the home-coming queen!"

Her father just looked at her. He seemed concerned. He wasn't impressed. "Debbi," he said, "you've got to learn to fail." And he didn't go to the homecoming.

Debbi married at 20. Then she got an idea: a fresh-baked cookie business. Hadn't the family always loved her cookies?

Mom shook her head. She couldn't understand why Debbi wanted to spend her life standing over an oven. Randy's parents said the plan would flop.

Some flop! Today Debbi is president and CEO of Mrs. Fields Cookies, with some 450 stores.

But the family still hasn't caught on. Her mom still worries, imagines people getting tired of Debbi's cook-ies, of her going broke. No one ever told her they were proud of her.

Came the day when Dad lay dying. Debbi sat on the edge of his bed and asked him for the last time if he was proud of her.

"Listen, Debbi," he said, "I love you just as much as I love everybody else. You're all special to me. I have no favorites."

But after the funeral, her sister Marlene showed her the photos from her father's wallet. Dino, his dog. The five girls with Mom. And one of Debbi at 17—just Debbi.

Now, says Debbi Fields, she keeps that photograph in her wallet, alongside a picture of her father.

I know how Debbi felt. Her father reminds me of my father. My dad was born in Stockholm. As an early teen he went off to sea and sailed the world—first in sailing ships, later in steam vessels. Twice he rounded Cape Horn.

One day his ship sailed down to Port Adelaide, in southern Australia. When it went on, Dad wasn't on board; he'd decided to stay. Eventually he married an Oz girl—pretty, dark-eyed, high-spirited. And they raised a family. Nine. I was the youngest.

I remember Dad as a loving father and husband, a sincere Christian. My first memory of him is the same as the last—early in the morning, sitting at the table, reading his Bible.

But he found it hard to praise. Praise, he feared, would turn your head. So although I earned the top grades in school and got the prize on parents' night, Dad just couldn't bring himself to say "Well done! I'm proud of you, Bill." His eyes shone, and I knew he was proud, but he couldn't express it.

Seems to me that the hunger for the father's blessing is very ancient. Way back in the book of Genesis we hear Esau's bitter cry after his conniving brother, Jacob, had stolen his birthright: "Bless me—me too, my father!" (Gen. 27:34, NIV).

We each tend to rerun our family relationships. If we grow up in a family of huggers, we hug our children. If we never hear our parents tell us we are special and can be something in life, we never tell our kids how much they mean to us.

Part of the change that the Lord calls us to, I believe, is in how we do things in the family. By His grace we need to do some things differently, break the cycle, start new traditions.

For everyone needs the father's blessing. And the mother's.

We all need to hear that we are special.

We all need to hear that we can make a difference.

We all need to hear we have an eternal future in God's plan.

We all need to hear parents commit themselves to help make the dream become reality.

We all need to be held and hugged.

Is it any surprise that Jesus' most famous story closes like this?

"So he got up and went to his father. But while he was still a long way off, his father saw him and was filled with compassion for him; he ran to his son, threw his arms around him and kissed him. The son said to him, 'Father, I have sinned against heaven and against you. I am no longer worthy to be called your son.' But the father said to his servants, 'Quick! Bring the best robe and put it on him. Put a ring on his finger and sandals on his feet. Bring the fattened calf and kill it. Let's have a feast and celebrate. For this son of mine was dead and is alive again; he was lost and is found.' So they began to celebrate" (Luke 15:20-24, NIV).

CHAPTER 8

Grandfather Painter

I never met my grandfather Painter, but I knew him. Grandfather Painter had a mountain named after him.

My mother was the youngest of his 10, and I am the youngest of her nine. So her father, Charles Painter, had lived a full life and passed away before I came along.

I used to look at his photograph, framed on the mantelpiece over the fireplace. Keen blue eyes. Short pointed beard. Intelligent. Arresting.

Grandfather Painter was a bastion in the community. A devout Anglican, he sang every Sunday in the choir of St. Andrews, up on the hill from our home by the river.

And Grandfather Painter had a mountain named after him. You could see it on the map, there in the Flinders Ranges—"Mount Painter."

Not a high mountain. Australia has no high mountains. Only a couple thousand feet. But a peak higher than those around it in the Flinders. And named after my grandfather.

Mother loved to tell the story of Mount Painter. As I think back over my growing-up years in South Australia, they echo and ring with the tale of her father and Mount Painter.

A century and more ago a survey party had set out from Adelaide, capital city of the young colony of South Australia. Its goal: to find a route through the Flinders Ranges, rugged and uninhabited, for the railway.

Grandfather Painter went along. He did the blacksmithing.

Deep in the Flinders the party got lost. They were off the map. They were making the map! The Flinders may not be high, but they have the wild, parched, haunting beauty of the outback. A beauty that kills lost travelers.

Among the unnamed peaks surrounding the party, one rose higher than the rest. Grandfather Painter volunteered to climb it in an effort to find a way out of the Flinders. He scaled the peak, spent that night at the summit, figured the route to take, and led the party to safety.

So they named the mountain after him.

Mother's story had another twist—a touch of the bizarre, the spooky. When Grandfather was atop his mountain, he noticed strange-looking rocks that glowed in the dark. He brought down a sack full of them and took them back to Adelaide, where they were kept for years in the care of Her Majesty's government in the Department of Mines.

Bizarre? Not so bizarre. A half century after Grandfather's climb uranium was discovered on—you guessed it—Mount Painter. Mount Painter grew from a pinpoint on the map to a star as the site of the first uranium mine in Oz.

Another bizarre twist. During my final year of study in industrial chemistry, I worked in the lab for the Department of Mines. One day my boss asked me to analyze a batch of ore that had just arrived—from Mount Painter.

I touched those stones and saw Grandfather Painter scaling a rugged peak while anxious colleagues waited below.

Mount Painter. It almost had my own name on it!

I never met my grandfather Painter, but I knew him. Wrong. I thought I knew him, but I didn't. My sister Gwen set me straight.

Gwen, who has published books, articles, and plays under the nom de plume Gwenda Painter, loves to research. One of her books explored the paddle wheeler era—not in the United States, but in Oz. Gwen got going on the early days of South Australia, founded in 1834. She traced the Painter clan to the first settlers and worked forward to the close of the nineteenth century.

And found a big problem. Dates. Right story, wrong man.

The peak in the Flinders was named after a Painter, but his name was John, not my grandfather. And Mount Painter was named in the 1850s, way too early for Charles to have been the savior-figure in the story. Charles did go with a survey party years later.

At first we didn't believe Gwen. We didn't *want* to believe her.

We didn't tell Mother. By then she was in her 80s and starting on the long descent. Mother wouldn't have believed Gwen. Mother couldn't have coped with this newfangled interpretation of history. She had seen her father climbing the mountain before I came on the scene.

But how did it begin—this mixing of man and event? How did the lore get started?

Grandfather Painter? I doubt it. I doubt that the bastion of church and community made up a tale to steal the glory from his relative.

Mother? Never! Hers was the pride of a believer.

Then how? In the garbling of facts and possibility, of inferences and imagination, reality and dreams. A story from long ago. A name dear to the ear. And the players—who could have set everyone straight—had passed off the stage.

Maybe Mother garbled facts and dreams. Maybe a relative did, and Mother picked up the story, put the pieces together, made it her own.

Every retelling made the story more real.

Moral? Beware of oral histories. The mind is tricky, and memory is deceitful. Good people can get their facts skewed, and sincerity of belief doesn't take the place of facts.

Or does it? Which was more real: the story Mother told and retold, or the story Gwen told?

Does it even matter?

I think it does.

Because what we are dealing with is more than Grandfather Painter and his spooky mountain. We are dealing with Jesus of Nazareth and the stories Christians have told about Him for nearly 2,000 years.

Those stories—myth or reality? The garbling of the facts, embellishing them with wonder and mystery, or a story that happened?

Which is to ask: Who *was* Jesus—a product of

imagination, or the Man of wonder, the Unique?

For most of this century a major school of New Testament study emphasized myths, imagination, the community, and oral history. These scholars told us that we couldn't recover the historical Jesus—the *real* Jesus—but only the Christ of faith in the minds of early Christians.

Their arguments were impressive, their footnotes endless.

And they were wrong.

The Gospels were written from first-person accounts. Matthew was one of Jesus' disciples. So was John. Luke tells us he consulted the eyewitnesses (Luke 1:1-4). Mark got his facts from Peter. Mark's Gospel, in fact, came out within 30 years or so of Jesus' death. There were plenty of people around to correct it, to expose it, if it were not true to the facts.

I never met my grandfather Painter. I thought I knew him, but I was wrong.

The Gospel writers met Jesus or met His closest followers. They knew Him, and they were right.

CHAPTER 9

The Yellow Tree

Yesterday I saw the yellow tree. After 15 years I saw it again—the yellow tree.

It took me two nights sitting up in airplanes and a six-hour trip over murderous roads to get to see the yellow tree. Well—I did have other business, but secretly I hoped to see the yellow tree again.

For 12 years—12 good years, happy years—I taught at Spicer College in India. Most of my classes met in a corner room on the second floor of the administration building. It looked down over the lawn where the yellow tree grew.

India is a hot country. The school year at Spicer College runs June through March, but we plunged immediately into summer school. And April is scorching hot.

Some Aprils hit 100 degrees Fahrenheit or higher every single day. The sun drills through your shirt, lacerating your back. Your head swims in the brightness. Your brain sizzles. Life retreats into summer hibernation. Dogs creep silently. Only mad dogs go out in the midday sun. (The Englishmen have all left.) A heat pall hangs in the air. The color green disappears.

Life in India is a gift of the monsoon. Every year it comes back, making its way northward. Day by day the cloud blanket advances, bringing storms, floods, relief from the inferno, and new life.

The monsoon line hits Sri Lanka in May, passes through southern India, and reaches Bombay around June 6. North of the line the land is a moonscape, south of it a garden.

Farther and farther north the line advances, hits the Himalayas, and begins to retreat. By October it has gone, left the map, vanished.

Some years not a drop of rain fell in Pune between the end of the monsoon in early October and its return the following June. Day by day the air grew drier, until humidity fell to only a scant percent and noses bled. Day by day the land gave up its moisture until it cracked open, gasping for life.

And day by day the mercury rose. By mid-March temperatures hit the mid-90s, by end-March the century.

Oh, the joy of summer school! No air-conditioning. Windows open to catch a breath of air, but catching instead dust clouds stirred up by the blast from the pit.

And through the open window—the yellow tree. It bloomed in April. The hotter the year, the drier the year, the greater the profusion of yellow blossoms. In a very dry year, not a leaf, only color. Only yellow against the gray of the earth.

I wanted to see my tree again. I wanted to see my sign of hope.

First night, Frankfurt. Second night, Bombay.

Spewed from the 747's bowels onto the Bombay sidewalk at 3:30 a.m. Hours of waiting, then across the coastal flats and up the Western Ghats to the Deccan Plateau, fighting trucks and hairpin bends.

To Pune. Spicer College—after 15 years. We arrived at 7:30 that night, showered quickly, and hurried to the meeting. Two thousand people gathered in a *shami-ana* (marquee) pitched on the lawn. Just across I could see the administration building and the corner room where I had taught religion classes.

It was 11:00 before the meeting let out, and my body felt like it was floating away from me. But I went hunting. And found it. Larger now, but even after 15 years still small.

The yellow tree. Long green pods hung from its branches. Many pods.

The yellow tree must have festooned the campus that past April.

If I ever start a club, it will be for optimists. The sign on the door will read: "All fears abandon ye who enter here."

And its name will be The Yellow Tree.

CHAPTER 10

Walking With Kings

S eest thou a man diligent in his business? he shall stand before kings; he shall not stand before mean men" (Prov. 22:29).

That "mean" isn't Scrooge-mean, but obscure-mean. And although I won't claim diligence in business, I have walked with kings and precious few mean chaps. For two years Noelene and I walked with King Myrl.

King Myrl met us on the platform of the Dehra Dun railway station in north India. Only a week before, we had arrived in India, fresh and green as cabbages. The "brethren" bought us sleeping rolls and a water jug. They filled the jug with boiled water and gave us a hamper of food. They took us to Bombay and got us tickets on the Dehra Dun express. They put us in a compartment for two and told us to lock the door and not open up for anyone until we got to Dehra Dun.

For two days and two nights the Dehra Dun Express plowed north. By day we gazed out the window at paddy fields and parched lands, hamlets and cities, temples

45

and mosques. We drank boiled water and ate from the hamper. By night we unrolled the beds and dreamed of Dehra Dun and the mountains.

The Dehra Dun Express screeched, ground, rumbled, squeaked, and rolled. New Delhi. On toward the mountains. Grinding up the Swallocks, into the Dun Valley, then laboring up the long incline. Outside the mountains came close—huge, massive, towering.

Dehra Dun. End of the line. And a tall man stands on the platform. Thin, almost gaunt. He spots us and hurries to meet us.

King Myrl.

Myrl O. Manley was a man without guile, a name that a shame never was connected with. He looked you straight in the eye. He stood straight. He walked straight.

For two years Noelene and I walked with King Myrl. High above Dehra Dun, 7,000 feet up but still only on the first ridge of the Himalayas, we lived and worked at Vincent Hill School. Myrl was its principal. I was boys' dean and Bible teacher. Noelene was music teacher and also matron for the small boys, who ranged from 8 to 18.

Myrl Manley ran a tight school. He made it one of the best the church had. Young people came to it from India, Ceylon, Pakistan, and Burma. Also from the Middle East, the Far East, and Africa. Some heard of it in the States and came.

Myrl never slept. He took the chapels, handled the finances, operated the press, supervised the garden, oversaw the food industry. Nothing happened at Vincent Hill School that Myrl didn't know about immediately. Or sooner.

Myrl didn't smile a lot. But students and staff respected and loved him. He looked awful serious, but he wanted the best for us all.

On one occasion we went through the excitement and trauma of a General Conference inspection. Dr. Richard Hammill, accompanied by leaders from headquarters in Pune, was coming on campus.

On the day of the final evaluation, Dick Hammill gathered the faculty in Myrl's office. The door was shut, and we waited to hear how we measured up. Myrl stepped outside a moment and saw hanging on the door, ready for Hammill's exit, a pair of red panties. Without breaking stride he grabbed them and dropped them into his suit pocket.

Myrl soon knew who had hung the panties on the door and who had supplied them. But he never told the faculty about the incident. They would have demanded instant expulsion of the boy and girl. Instead he told just the girls' dean and me, and we handled the discipline privately.

I suspect Myrl knew some things he didn't tell even us.

After two years, King Myrl and Queen Betty returned to the United States. He served at Andrews University, and then as president of Union College. He retired, but kept on working. When Union College got into a mess, they called him back to clean it up.

Serving with distinction—Myrl O. Manley.

Honest. Straight. Upright.

A king.

We loved the work at Vincent Hill, but it had one drawback. Almost all the students were missionaries' kids. Noelene and I had come to serve India and her peoples, and we began to grow restless to be among them.

So after a couple of years at Vincent Hill School, we

asked "the brethren" if they could assign us to "the field."

They sent us to Spicer College.

Maliakal Eapen Cherian, only in his mid-thirties, had just been elected president.

We stayed 12 years at Spicer. We worked closely with Dr. Cherian and quickly came to realize that he is an individual with remarkable gifts.

He could have made his mark in the church or in society in a variety of fields. If he had stayed with theology—he was head of the Religion Department when appointed president—he most certainly would have become one of the church's leading theologians. He has a clear, philosophical mind, sharp in discernment, probing, relentless in logic.

Over the course of the years, Cherian has emerged as one of the leading Christians of India. *The* leading Christian, a longtime India hand told me. He is head of about 20 organizations (such as the YMCA) meaning he chairs the boards or serves in an honorary capacity. But Spicer College has been his life. He has poured himself into Spicer; Spicer and Cherian have become synonymous.

Cherian came to Spicer as a teenager, graduated, and immediately was taken onto the staff. That was in 1949. He stayed on till 1990, serving as dean of men, Bible teacher, department head, and—for 28 years—president.

Southern Asia follows a mandatory retirement policy, and in April 1990 Cherian received a letter from division headquarters announcing that the committee had voted his retirement. But in a startling turn of events, the Indianapolis General Conference session elected him president of the division. So as I write, the

Cherian connection continues: although no longer president of Spicer, he chairs her board.

I was one of Cherian's first appointments as president. Those years at Spicer were intense. We worked long hours, but no one worked longer than our chief. He had a dream, and we all caught it. He visioned a college that would hold high her head in the academic world, one that would give a lead to the educators of India.

India follows the British system of education, which means that all tertiary education comes under the universities. Colleges follow the curriculum handed out by the universities, which set and grade the examinations. The only way to academic recognition is to join the system.

But Dr. Cherian's dream for Spicer ran along different paths. Spicer would follow her own curriculum. It would include required courses in religion and a compulsory work program. Spicer would have to achieve academic standing the hard way: by a unique curriculum that commanded respect because of the excellence of its product.

It was a bold vision, but we dreamed the impossible dream along with our president. And gradually the breakthroughs came. First Pune University began to accept Spicer graduates on an individual merit basis for graduate work. As they proved competent, the doors opened wider. Scores of Spicer graduates have earned master's degrees or the Ph.D. in a variety of fields.

Then Spicer College introduced graduate programs of her own. Working through Andrews University, Spicer offers master's programs in religion, education, and business.

I sat in a large public meeting celebrating the

seventy-fifth anniversary of Spicer. Speaker after speaker—the mayor of Pune, the vice-chancellor of Pune University, leaders of industry and government—rose to congratulate Spicer for the uniqueness of her curriculum and the quality of her graduates. And over and over they praised the one whose vision and energy had made it happen.

Once, many years ago when Cherian was a student, he wore the white Gandhi cap, badge of free India. The missionaries who at that time ran the school took him aside and remonstrated with him.

And years later when in a surprise move the Spicer College board chose him to lead the college, others shook their heads. Under national leadership the college would go to the dogs.

But the person they chose was no "mean" man. This dreamer, this man sure of himself and sure of Spicer's place in India and in the divine plan, became its preeminent leader.

After India, the seminary; and after the seminary, the General Conference and the *Adventist Review*.

The General Conference is a great place to work, but in some measure it partakes of the spirit of Washington. Which means politics.

That was a new ball game for me. At times I felt like I was walking in a minefield.

I turned to a close friend. Whom could he recommend for advice? With hardly a moment's hesitation he responded, "The wisest person in the General Conference is Elder Charles Bradford. Why don't you talk to him?"

I did. My friend was right: "Brad" is rich in sound counsel.

Brad and I became close. For 10 years we worked together. As the North American Division came into its own and its leaders sought a vehicle to help bind the division together, we reshaped the monthly *Review* so that more and more it serves as the division paper, supplied free to every home.

I love this man.

He is, I believe, one of the great assets of the Seventh-day Adventist Church. Brad is himself, unfettered by the chains of self-importance that too many Adventist ministers and leaders drag around behind them. He is an individual, unique, a person redeemed by Jesus Christ and set free to glorify Him by being just Brad.

And how big is that "just"!

There is none like Brad anywhere in the church— not in North America, not overseas.

None like him in his power of spontaneous anecdote, appropriate to the occasion, diffusing tension, piercing gobbledygook and pretense.

None like him in his ability to sway a meeting of "the brethren" by the power of his logic and the passion of his convictions.

None like him in preaching the Word, uplifting the Master, building up men and women in the privileges and responsibilities of membership in the church.

Brad is a kind person. No bitterness, no sharp edge, no festering wound, no smoldering hurt drives him on.

His career for the Master stretched wider and wider, higher and higher, reaching its apogee, not in his election to the presidency of the North American Division, but in his final year of service.

Boldly he spoke his convictions concerning the direction for North America. With telling persuasiveness he outlined the biblical arguments for the full empowerment of women to the gospel ministry.

Then he walked away. Walked away without apology or whining, without regret or pining. Walked away applauded, feted, admired, respected, loved.

About a year before the 1990 General Conference session, Noelene got an idea. Brad had announced his plan to retire, announced it and stuck with it in spite of pleas to continue or even hints that he should be the next General Conference president.

"What a treasure the church has in Brad!" said Noelene. "Why don't we collect his anecdotes and words of wisdom and put them in a book, ready for his retirement?"

Great idea—another one from Noelene's fertile mind. We sounded out the Review and Herald Publishing Association, and they jumped at the plan. But—they needed the finished manuscript in four months!

It was a struggle, but a wonderful one. I ended up spending hours talking with Brad, getting him primed, while the tape recorder ran. Brad's nephew, Dr. Calvin Rock, came through with pages of suggestions for anecdotes, sayings, and sermons.

The whole effort was voluntary. Noelene and I donated all royalties to Brad's project for researching the history of the Sabbath in Africa. Secretaries donated their time to type the manuscript. Brad's assistant, Gary Patterson, helped coordinate efforts.

Anyone who knows Brad would be glad to do the same. He's a king.

I can see him reading this and saying to Ethel, "Just look at what they've written about me. Bill has gone too far with all this stuff!"

So, enough of this stuff. Let Brad have the last word.

Here is one of his favorite anecdotes, and my favorite:

"The Johnstown Flood was the greatest natural disaster of American history. Walls of water, tons and tons, thousands upon thousands of gallons, rushed down and swept everything away. Few people survived.

"This brother survived and forever after he told the story. It became *his* story. I suppose he embellished it. After having told it at conventions and wherever you must tell stories, he gets to heaven and tells St. Peter, 'Please, I want to tell the story of the Johnstown Flood.'

"The crowd is excited. Peter says, 'You may, but remember, Noah is in the audience'" *(The Wit & Wisdom of Charles Bradford,* compiled by William and Noelene Johnsson, p. 104).

In Washington my work brought me into close association with someone else whom I soon recognized as a no "mean" man.

Elder Neal C. Wilson knew me before I knew him.

We first met in 1975 on the campus of Andrews University, shortly after Noelene and I had come from India. I saw him approaching and recognized him; I knew he would not know who I was. But he walked up to me, put out his hand, and said, "Hello, Bill, how are you?"

Wilson's ability to remember faces, names, and personal details is extraordinary—unparalleled in my experience. This gift, which he must have cultivated, stems from a deep interest in people. On the personal level, he is warm and unhurried. During Wilson's term as General Conference president it sometimes took you weeks to get to see him, but he would never cut short the visit.

His encyclopedic, computer-precise brain masters

agendas and issues. After Neal Wilson surveys a matter, going around pros, cons, and options, every base has been covered.

I think that history will recall this man of many gifts as not only a strong leader but an outstanding one— one of the Adventist greats.

He led the world church for nearly 12 years. His centralized, activist style thrived on problem solving. The range of concerns through which he guided the church is startling in scope, variety, and lasting impact.

Wilson presided over the first major restudy of SDA beliefs in nearly 50 years, culminating in the adoption of the 27 fundamental beliefs at the Dallas General Conference session in 1980. These statements are a theological landmark for Adventists.

During his years as General Conference vice president for North America, Wilson put himself on the line in favor of the full participation of Blacks in the life and work of the church. As president of the world church, he continued to press for a community of equality and justice.

"It's harvesttime," he declared as he assumed the mantle of the GC presidency. Growth became the watchword of the next 12 years: Adventists stretched toward a goal of 1,000 accessions per day, reached it, went beyond, and now have passed 1,500 a day.

Wilson confronted a series of major problems— challenges to Adventist understanding of prophecy and the heavenly sanctuary, and to Ellen White's writings; and financial crises in the Davenport investments and the bankruptcy of Harris Pine Mills. But he refused to be deterred: resilient and tenacious, he pressed on.

Wilson was quick to grasp the potential of the mass media for propagating the Adventist faith. Under his direction the church established the far-reaching short-wave radio outreach in Guam, and embarked on a similar scheme for Italy.

The Wilson presidency spelled out the role and function of the General Conference and its divisions, cleared the way for full division status for North America, and, in a major reorganization, combined five departments into one—Church Ministries. Likewise he led in restructuring the church in Africa, Europe, and Southern Asia.

Although Wilson is not an academic, he is comfortable among scholars. He fostered research, high-tech medicine, gathering of data, and input from experts in the church's decision-making.

As NAD and GC president, Wilson encouraged a greater role for women in the work of the church, opening doors for women to serve in gospel ministry and as local church elders.

Always looking ahead, Elder Wilson pointed the way for the nineties—a global strategy for global mission.

Beyond these individual accomplishments, however, Wilson functioned as a world leader. He is as much at home in Africa, India, or South America as in the United States. He represented the church with dignity and grace as he met heads of state. He is wise with the wisdom that comes from loving people as a people.

We worked together in the ministry of the *Adventist Review*. As chairman of the *AR* editorial board he gave me counsel, but he did not try to interfere in running the church paper. Although he did not always agree with everything we put in print, he supported the *Review* and staff privately and in public.

In September 1988 I stood atop Mount Kilimanjaro

with Neal Wilson. The climb up was tough, exhausting. I admired the spirit of this man who sets his face unrelentingly toward the goal.

He left the General Conference presidency at age 70. But like Moses, his eye is not dimmed or his strength abated.

Manley, Cherian, Bradford, Wilson. I have walked with kings. I have been privileged, blessed beyond desert, beyond measure.

Some people won't like this part of the book. Some people have criticized savagely each of the individuals I have described.

And these kings have their weaknesses. They made mistakes. But they have done great things for the Lord and His people, and I don't hesitate to honor them. They will be lauded at their funerals; I prefer to give the bouquets while they still live.

I could mention other kings, but enough is enough.

One area of omission stands out, however. No women. Not even one.

The people in this chapter were my colleagues, my bosses. I have worked under the direction of leaders of other race, but not under a woman.

The Seventh-day Adventist Church has been slow to open her administration to women. I'm sorry for that. I hope change will come soon.

For the church's nobility includes women. A woman—a great woman—helped found this movement. Great women have sustained and nurtured her, and extended her borders. Great women today speed onward her message.

I think of so many.

And of one in particular.

But to write of her—that one who has so blessed my life and the church—calls for another chapter.

Indeed a whole book.

CHAPTER 11

Gracious Giver, Gracious Gift

C hristmas still turns me on. Given its crass commercialization in our times, that's no small feat. Want to see a sad mess of human pottage? Just visit any department store on Christmas Eve. Robotlike creatures wander by the piles of riffled garments; glassy-eyed assistants ring up sales and wait for release from human bondage. Everything spells *jaded*—jaded customers, jaded kids, jaded clerks.

Christmas turns life into one huge bazaar. Whatever happened to Christ?

I used to enjoy that old song "The Twelve Days of Christmas." That was before some wiseacre began computing for me something I didn't need to know—what a partridge in a pear tree would cost today, along with two turtledoves, right through eight maids a-milking to 12 drummers drumming. So every year I have to suffer these smart-aleck calculations, item by item, until they get to the grand total in dollars and cents.

Give me the three French hens, and forget about the money.

Jesus said: "It is more blessed to give than to receive" (Acts 20:35). Does anyone still believe that? Even Christians?

December brings many people heartburn instead of blessing. They not only have to buy the expected gifts, but they have to get them at just the right level. If they're too cautious, their office workers will think they're stingy; if they go overboard, they can seem uppity.

And those party games in which everyone shows up with a gift (specified value, of course—keep it to $10) and you exchange or grab from someone else to get what you want bring out plain old-fashioned greed.

I have a dream—a Christmas without cash registers, Visa, or MasterCard. A Christmas during which no one figures out how much he or she ought to spend on a gift. A Christmas during which no one calculates how much someone paid for his or her gift.

I remember, dimly, the first Christmas gifts I ever bought. It was a long time ago, and I cannot tell you where I got the money for the gifts. Not that my gifts cost very much that Christmas.

I remember going to the little store at the end of our street and spending all I had. The process took some time: We were a large family, and I had to be sure I could get something for each of my eight brothers and sisters (all older) plus my parents. I bought—candy! Chocolates, as I recall—different sorts, different sizes, chocolate coins wrapped in gold paper.

Then returning back down the street, wrapping the gifts, and placing a name card for each. And on Christmas morning, what fun!

And what love. What grace!

My mother spent most of the year getting ready for Christmas, it seemed. Certainly by July and August we'd find her knitting or crocheting, looking ahead to December 25.

Christmas Day she gave us each a gift from her own hand. Later each child and his or her spouse received a gift. Still later, each grandchild. Eventually each great-grandchild.

That was giving. *That* was love. *That* was grace.

When God gave us His Gift of gifts, He gave His own. His best. He cleaned out heaven for us.

And He gave Him to us forever. In taking our nature, the Saviour has bound Himself to humanity by a tie that is never to be broken. A gift is forever.

God, the gracious giver, gave *before* we gave to Him. He gave to us in our wretchedness, our stubbornness, our waywardness.

He gave to us, not calculating our response. He gave to the one who spits upon the Gift as well as to one who embraces it.

God, the gracious receiver, delights in the gifts we bring to Him. Our paltry offerings—how miserable they are, how despicable! Yet they are all we have, and we give them in love. And He receives them—smiles on us, rejoices in our excitement, clasps us in fond embrace.

The world rushes by, but the Babe still lies in the manger. (And the manger, by the way, doesn't much resemble the scene in Macy's storefront window. Animals don't smell good; donkeys have bad breath; straw breeds fleas.)

But the Babe lies in the manger. A Gift. Perfect. Forever.

That's why Christmas still turns me on.

CHAPTER 12

Crystal

I don't like the center seat on airplanes. My long legs never quite find enough room, and I get a feeling of being hemmed in. But last Sunday I sat next to Crystal, and she gave me one of the pleasantest trips ever.

Must be a full plane, I mused to myself as I squeezed into seat E on Delta's Flight 585 from Portland, Maine, to Boston. The window seat was unoccupied—and inviting. But just before takeoff, a man hurried on board with a little girl. He showed her to her place.

"Give Daddy a kiss," he said, and he was gone.

Crystal.

All of 5, perhaps 6. White dress with purple ribbons. A colored bow on one shoe. Long dark hair. Sad eyes. A little bag with dolls and books sticking out.

Crystal fastened her seat belt. Then she began to stuff her dolls under the belt as well.

"What's his name?" I asked, pointing to a pink doll.

"Panther." She held up the doll.

"Of course. The Pink Panther."

"I have some books, too." She opened her bag. That's when I saw the name in large, uncertain block letters: CRYSTAL.

"Can you read, Crystal?"

"No, I'm too young."

By now the wheels were racing faster and faster, and the engines were roaring, and we were up in the sky.

"Look at the big lake down there—such a big lake," Crystal said.

"That's the ocean, Crystal."

So we talked about the ships down below and the clouds and how Crystal was on her way to Georgia, because every summer she came back to Maine to stay with her father.

Then: "I'm hungry. I didn't have any dinner yet." It was already 2:45 p.m.

And then: "Would you read to me?"

She selected the mouse book.

So we read about the mouse that went on a journey. Crystal followed the pictures and laughed now and then.

Then we read about the very tall mouse and the very small mouse.

After that, she wanted the mouse that had a bath and then the old mouse.

We were coming down. "Please, one more story," Crystal pleaded.

So we launched into the mouse that went sailing and just had the mouse safe on shore as the wheels touched the runway of Boston's Logan International Airport.

"I'm sorry, Crystal. I have to get off here to get

another plane to my home in Washington. You stay on this plane, and it will take you to Atlanta. And I think the flight attendant will bring you some food soon."

I *was* sorry. Although I had been on the road for nearly three weeks, I wished my ticket were marked Atlanta.

I gathered my coat and bag and began to make my way down the aisle. I looked back at a little girl in a pretty white dress with purple ribbons. The eyes were very sad. She waved.

Crystal.

Suddenly I felt angry. I felt angry that a little girl has to travel alone hundreds of miles every summer, angry that she sees her mother part of the year, and her daddy another part.

After meeting Crystal, I could readily become a crusader for children's rights.

Crystal didn't ask to come into this world. Crystal's *right* is a home where she can be loved by both parents and not have to shuttle back and forth alone.

No, I'm not arguing that divorce is always the wrong course. In some situations, such as child or spouse abuse, it is the lesser of two evils.

But my plea is this: How many men and women today think of the Crystals along with their own desires? When they grow tired of their companion, or find someone they like better, or "want out" from the pressures that come with maintaining a close relationship, do they consider what the breakup of the home will mean to Crystal?

Is anyone listening out there?

CHAPTER 13

Moving On

I turned 56, and I'm still trying to figure out what it means.

In our family there were always two Bills. My sister Bonnie was dating her Bill when I, eight children later and last of the line, came along. They named me for Bill.

So he was Bill, and I was Young Bill or Billie. Young Bills don't get old. Young Bills don't turn 56.

Reluctantly, gingerly, I begin to contemplate the possibility represented by the reverse of those numbers. I visit Oz, and friends from way back talk about their retirement plans, ask us about ours, and we have to give an answer.

Moving on is hard for many people. It's a male problem, because men tend to find their identity in their work. No job, and we men cease to be. A blob. A mass of Jell-O. Chopped liver.

Some stay on too long. Some wise up early enough and bow out gracefully.

At 56 it's easy to plan a graceful exit. Nine years later it may be harder to face.

For anyone interested in the topic, here are Johnsson's two laws of moving on.

Law Number One: Thou shalt not succeed in naming thy successor.

Try as we might to ensure a successor of our choosing—one to carry on our style—it won't work. The moment we announce retirement, power leaks away. Our opinion, our wish, no longer carries weight. And even if by some stratagem we install a successor, the reign of the new monarch likely will be brief.

Law Number Two: Thy successor will succeed in removing thy stamp from the work.

In Egypt there rose up a king who knew not Joseph. That's par for the course.

In Egypt, too, they produced one woman among the succession of monarchs. Hatshepsut. A powerful queen, we know now.

Historians took some time to find out about her. The monarch who succeeded her toppled her statues and chiseled her name out of the inscriptions.

That man had a problem.

Wising up about retirement tells us that moving on is like the course of the seasons. Fall follows summer, and by September we begin to look for the turning of the leaves and the long, cool nights. If September rings down and it's still hot, we feel out of rhythm.

Solomon, who told us about the time for so many things, could have added this one to set us straight: "There is a time for work, and a time for moving on."

Maybe he didn't wise up on his fifty-sixth birthday.

CHAPTER 14

The Man in the Bowler Hat

S cene: London, early afternoon in March. A couple with two small children enter a cafeteria. They select food, pay the cashier, and sit at a table.

Us. We're on our way back to India after a furlough/ study leave in the United States.

Enter: The Man in the Bowler Hat. A proper English gentleman. He tips his hat, greets the servers, others sitting at tables. The few people sitting around seem to recognize him. We don't.

The Man in the Bowler Hat selects a proper English poached egg, pays his bill, and looks for a table. He comes straight toward us. "May I join you?"

For the next 45 minutes, TMBH knife-and-forks his poached egg—and talks. Mainly talks. We put away our food and listen. Even the kids are fascinated. TMBH holds them spellbound.

TMBH tells us about the city of London. Not the sprawling metropolis of the tourist circuit, but the one-mile-square City of London at its heart.

He tells us about sights that the tourist never visits—St. Bartholomew's Hospital and St. Bartholomew's Church, built 900 years ago by Rahere, a court jester who saw the light. Of the weeping bust in St. Bartholomew's Church, legacy of a scholar who died friendless.

In the course of the conversation, TMBH reveals a little about himself. He qualifies for appointment as lord mayor of the City of London, but can't afford to accept the largely ceremonial post, which entails a succession of banquets, dinners, and public ceremonies.

But his love is the City, not himself. *His* city. He is full of the City of London.

Soon, too soon, it's time to go. The Man in the Bowler Hat gets up, tips his hat, and bids us good afternoon. He greets the cafeteria management and is gone.

We wander through the streets of the City of London, watching for places designated by our host. We pass Aldersgate Street, see a sign that marks the spot where John Wesley felt "strangely warmed" as he found the Lord.

Close by the Smithfield meat market we find it—the old church. The heavy door swings slowly as we step down from the street to enter St. Bartholomew's. (Over the centuries the pavement level has gradually built up.) A booklet by the entrance tells the story of Rahere and how he left the life of a fellow at court to establish the church and the hospital.

We browse through the old building, heavy with plaques and memorials. Yes, it's here too—the marble bust of the friendless Ph.D. No one wept at his death, but in the dark confines of St. Bartholomew's, the moisture condenses on the marble head and forms rivulets from the corners of the eyes.

Later, ensconced in our boarding house for the night, feeding coins into the gas space heater, we turn on the telly. There's been a bomb outrage—IRA terrorists struck this afternoon in London. They took the casualties, the newscaster tells us, to St. Bartholomew's Hospital.

The Man in the Bowler Hat gave us an unforgettable day in the City of London.

Who said that proper English gentlemen are stuffy? What of those jokes about two Englishmen shipwrecked on a desert island and waiting for someone to make the introductions?

Stereotypes are stuffy. Stereotypical Englishmen have to wait to be introduced.

Proper English gentlemen don't.

CHAPTER 15

Uncle Wilf

My uncle Wilf was a sainted man who drove like death. Everyone who knew him was sure of one thing: He would die with his boots on—behind the wheel.

Outside his automobile, no gentler or kinder soul walked the good earth. Uncle Wilf loved the Lord, the church, and his "Glo" (Auntie Gloria) in equal measure.

His eyes would shine as at family worship he boomed out his favorite hymn from the old SDA *Church Hymnal*: "Eternal Light! Eternal Light!/ How pure that soul must be/ When, placed within Thy searching sight,/ It shrinks not, but with calm delight/ Can live, and look on Thee." He was the only one I ever knew to choose that hymn—never did I hear it sung in a church service.

Devotedly he waited on Glo—running errands, ready to be her busboy, answering her every call.

He was a little man, Uncle Wilf, only a few inches past five feet and slightly built. But he worked ceaselessly—for Glo, in the garden, for the church. He had migrated to Australia as a young man and retained a strong English edge to his speech.

But behind the wheel: unadulterated murder. Not because he drove so fast, but because he drove so slow. Uncle Wilf, skilled as he was in the machine shop, was a menace on the road.

The whole time I knew him (only after I got involved with Noelene) he wore a hearing aid. As he grew older, his hearing decreased further. And Glo progressively lost her sight until she had only peripheral vision. She was legally blind.

So he would cruise along hearing nothing, and Glo would ride beside him, seeing nothing.

We would come home to Australia on furlough from India. We'd fly into Perth from Singapore, and it would always be 3:00 or 4:00 in the morning. Through immigration and customs and then to the sleepy-eyed crowd outside, dragging our luggage. Uncle Wilf would always be there, with Auntie Glo.

And then—the drive to their home. Which soon brought us wide awake.

One morning as we slid along (I kid you not), we were the only car on the road. The city lay silent, drugged in the last moments before the light. We could smell in the cool air the scent that Aussies recognize as soon as they come home from abroad—the faint, healing perfume of the eucalyptus trees.

We slid up to an intersection and stopped at the traffic light. We hadn't seen another car in miles. Uncle Wilf wanted to turn right, which meant—since they drive on the left in Oz—a turn across the traffic. If there had been any.

So Uncle Wilf waited to get the green arrow for the

right turn. He waited. He waited through an entire cycle of lights. The green arrow didn't come on. It didn't come on because he hadn't pulled into the turning lane to trigger the arrow.

We saw. We knew. But we kept quiet. At 5:00 a.m. after sitting up with your kids all night on an airplane, one is glad for silence.

So we waited. Eventually Uncle Wilf, patient saint though he was, had had enough. When the light came green again, he made his right turn.

Right in the path of a car coming the other way.

The car. The only car. I kid you not.

And that baby was coming at us! I mean, he was motoring; barreling down the empty highway at 5:00 a.m. when all the traffic cops had folded their machines for the night.

Uncle Wilf stopped in midstream. The night ranger hit everything he had and reined her in a couple coats of paint from us. We looked him right in the eye.

Then, without a word, Uncle Wilf put his car in gear, and we pulled away. Strangers in the night, and ever so glad to remain so.

No one said a word as we slid the rest of the way home.

Which helps explain why the Johnsson family showed little relish for a picnic trip or an excursion to the beach. Waving off Auntie's protestations, we rode the bus into Perth to go shopping.

Even the kids, who at that age despised walking, fell in love with terra firma.

And we counted the days to Sabbath. Church was only a couple miles away, but that was plenty of space for major damage.

During one visit Auntie's insistence couldn't be

denied. We would take a spin to Fremantle, the port city for Perth. So we piled in and Uncle Wilf took off. Come Fremantle, and as we negotiated a curve, Uncle Wilf took the shortest route.

Which meant he cut across the lanes.

Which meant he cut off a VW bugful of young men.

They tooted and shouted behind us. Then they tooted and shouted as they drove up alongside us.

But Uncle Wilf kept straight on. He saw only the road ahead and heard nothing. Auntie Glo beside him saw nothing. And in the back seat we were trying to do the disappearing trick.

After a couple hours at the beach, we started back home. On a side street we passed a parked VW bug. And an amazing thing happened: the occupants began to shout at us and shake their fists.

All of which passed by Uncle Wilf, driving straight ahead, and Auntie Glo sitting beside him.

Only the Johnssons were trying to melt into the back seat.

My uncle Wilf! Whatever else you may have concluded about him, please remember this: He was a dear man. I loved him. I miss him.

Yes, he is gone. He died with his boots on—but not, as we all expected, behind the wheel. He died at 86, in the store at the end of their street where he had walked to get something for his beloved Glo. He just dropped in his tracks. It was all over like that—no pain, no struggle.

So two things I learned from knowing Uncle Wilf.

If any of God's people make it through to the eternal kingdom, Uncle Wilf will be one of them.

And in that kingdom we won't drive automobiles.

CHAPTER 16

Kit Bag

On a shimmering summer day, three Ozzie lads set off for the beach. Lennie and I, and Lennie's cousin. Lennie, the biggest, lived on the corner of our street. His cousin, youngest and smallest, had come from the country to spend the holidays with Lennie. He was a joker, always scheming up a trick; you never knew when he was serious.

We gathered together our swim shorts and towels, and threw them into a kit bag. The kit bag was made of leather, with a handle, and was shaped like an oversize lunch pail.

I haven't seen one in years, but ages ago everybody had a kit bag. A popular song of those years told you to pack your problems in a kit bag and smile them away.

The beach was 10 or 12 miles distant. We caught a trolley in the center of our hometown, Adelaide, and then another that took us to the beach.

Once there we changed, stowed our clothes and money in the kit bag, and plunged in. All afternoon we swam and played, ducked each other, threw a ball back and forth in the light shimmering on the water.

Lennie's cousin was first to quit. We let him go and resumed tossing the ball.

After a while we heard him shouting to us from the sand. We couldn't hear what he was saying, but he was waving his arms around.

Another trick! We turned back to the water and went on playing.

But he kept on shouting and waving, and reluctantly we left the water, feeling put out at his antics.

"What's the matter with you?" we called out as we reached the shallow water.

"The kit bag—it's gone!"

We didn't believe him. This was a really weak one. He'd pay for it!

But after we'd looked all around the open beach where we'd left the kit bag, plus behind every bush on the grass higher up, where Lennie's cousin might have hidden it, we changed our minds.

No kit bag.

No towels.

No clothes.

No money.

Three Ozzie lads marooned on a shimmering summer afternoon.

We did the only thing we could think of—headed for the police station. The officer's eyes raked our faces as we told the story. Then—"Wait here." He disappeared into an adjoining room.

When he came back, he had in his hand—a kit bag!

Eagerly we opened it. There were our towels and clothes. Even the money for our fare home.

We looked on the officer with wonder shining in our

eyes. Then he told us a story.

No, he wasn't Mandrake the magician. A woman had been lying on a blanket on the grass, dozing in the shimmering light. Out of the corner of her eye she saw a hand snatch her purse. She sat up and shouted, "Stop, thief! Stop, thief! He took my purse."

Someone gave chase, then a policeman. They apprehended him.

And he was carrying a kit bag.

"Your kit bag?" they asked him at the station.

He swore it was.

Then why was it filled with boys' clothes?

The officer gave us back the clothes and money, but kept the kit bag. "We need this as evidence," he told us. "And you boys must come back here next Tuesday at 9:00. Be sure to bring the clothes and towels with you."

Next Tuesday we were up early and back to the beach, our clothes and towels under our arm in a bundle. We sat in the little courtroom and waited for the magistrate to call us. At last it came: The police brought out the kit bag filled with our clothes. We testified that we were the lawful owners.

There he stood—the man who'd stolen our kit bag. Stereotype of the petty thief. Shifty eyes. Furtive look. He had been released from jail only a few days before. He would go back for another 18 months.

Case complete. We took the kit bag and headed back to the city.

I never saw Lennie's cousin after that summer. Lennie and I haven't seen each other for many years.

In a manner I did not dream of on that shimmering summer day, the world has opened up to me like an oyster. I have swum in the beaches of the Pacific and the Atlantic, in the Arabian Sea and the Bay of Bengal, on the coast of the Caribbean and the coast of Chile. I have walked on the sands of Goa, which scorched my feet even at Christmas, the coolest season of the year, and have joined the Swedes soaking in the pale May sun of the Northlands.

And the little man, where is he?

The little man with the shifty eyes and the furtive look—what have the years brought him? Does he yet live? If he does, is he in jail again?

Life, it sometimes seems, is like a treadmill. Day follows day in unbroken, never-ceasing succession. On a shimmering summer day life will go on forever.

We could almost believe it—except for the kit bag.

CHAPTER 17

Ellen

I never had hang-ups about Ellen White. I discovered her for myself, and she showed me Jesus.

I wasn't brought up in a home where I kept hearing "Mrs. White says you shouldn't . . ." "Mrs. White says you should . . ." The red books were there in the home, lined up in the bookcase that stood in the hallway. Dad would get them out and read them. I saw him reading them. But he never turned them on me.

Maybe he did with the older kids. I don't know. I was the youngest, and Mother hadn't become an Adventist, and by the time I came along the wars of religion had all been fought and a truce declared. Under the terms of peace, religion would be the one subject ruled out of discussion.

So Dad went to church and taught his Sabbath school class. He studied his Bible and read the *Signs of the Times* and the *Australasian Record*. He said the grace at meals, which always went: "For what we are about to receive may the Lord make us truly thankful.

Amen." And he brought out Ellen White's books and read them to himself.

Mother went to church. Occasionally. The Anglican Church.

My brothers and sisters went to church. Occasionally. The Anglican Church.

Sometime when I was 10 or 11 Dad got me to start reading the Bible. Just to read, cover to cover, Genesis to Revelation. Then to read it again. And again. And again.

It was the best habit I ever formed. It has stayed with me for life. It has been, probably, the most important influence in my life.

No matter why a person starts reading the Bible, I believe that if he or she keeps reading, the Bible will bring new life, new creation.

That happened to me.

I began to talk to Dad about the Bible. I began to ask him questions. I wanted to know what "Selah" meant in the Psalms.

Dad knew the Bible and the Lord of the Bible. Step by step he nurtured the new creation. I wonder, now, how much prayer also went into that new life.

I had become a Christian. Born again. Praying. Believing. Feeding on the Word.

Not attending church. Not baptized. But a Christian.

Enter Ellen.

I don't recall how I got started on her writings. If Dad introduced her—and I expect he did—it was so gentle, so low-key, that the incident didn't register.

Ellen's writings did.

I read myself through her works, and they showed me Jesus.

Steps to Christ led me to forgiveness.

The Desire of Ages helped me fall in love with the story of Jesus.

Christ's Object Lessons opened up His teachings.

Patriarchs and Prophets opened up the Old Testament, revealing Jesus.

The Great Controversy opened up the last events leading to His return.

Ellen was never a club or a killjoy to me. I can understand—grasp mentally—how some people brought up on Ellen White have grown up hating her. I can understand, but I cannot enter that experience.

And my advice to those people, like my advice to people wanting to know about Adventists and what we think of Ellen, is: Read her. Read *Steps to Christ*. Read *The Desire of Ages*. Read *Christ's Object Lessons*. Read *Patriarchs and Prophets*. Read *The Great Controversy*.

Forget about Canright, or Walter Rea, or what the Church of Christ people write about her.

Just read her.

That, after all, is the only fair and sure test of her writings.

And of Ellen.

I think the Adventist Church still has a long way to go in coming to terms with Ellen. Our pioneers had a struggle; and the struggle goes on.

Some in her day wanted no part of her counsel.

Just like today.

Some in her day wanted to raise her writings to a level equal with Scripture, searching her words to explain Scripture rather than searching Scripture itself.

Just like today.

I suppose there always will be a continuum.

Some Adventists will tend toward the pole of equating her writings with Scripture; others to the pole of limiting their value to her own time.

I think we need to learn to live with these differences of perspective. To accept each other with these differences.

Just as she learned and accepted them in her day.

I wish we could set up two boundary markers. And keep hammering them in.

Boundary marker 1: Ellen's writings are *not* Scripture, never to be equated with Scripture, but always tested by Scripture.

Boundary marker 2: Her writings are inspired, of continuing value to the church.

I think these markers could be of enormous help in clarifying the role of Ellen to the world. And to ourselves.

A prophetic gift brings such blessing in the hands of God. But it can bring confusion as people misuse it.

Years ago, when arguments over Ellen's "borrowing" reached a crescendo, the General Conference put me on a committee to study the evidence. We were treated to an onslaught of examples, some convincing, some dubious.

Dr. Fred Veltman, a New Testament scholar, was on the committee. After more than a day's exposure of Ellen's "plagiarism," some of the others were amazed that Fred and I (who also specialized in New Testament) seemed unimpressed.

Why? Fred and I had been through it all before, and in a more threatening arena, with higher stakes. We had studied the Gospels in doctoral seminars, had seen the surprising similarities and equally surprising differences in the accounts of Jesus' life and teachings. Had seen, pondered, and come to terms with the evidence.

I don't think we can fully understand the nature of inspired writings. On one hand, they are so human. Faulty spelling. Faulty grammar. Inadequate expression. On the other hand, they are so divine. They breathe and pulsate with Heaven's power, Heaven's life.

To me, they show the great condescension.

God takes human form. God limits Himself.

Just like Jesus.

The Scriptures show this divine-human quality.

So does Ellen.

CHAPTER 18

Morning

Gather up the stones, you slugabeds, for I have a confession to make. I am a morning person. In fact, I'm a *morning* morning person. I get up early, no matter what hour I retire for the night. And if I have work to do, I get up very early.

Much of my writing—and I think my best writing—has come in the early morning. Probably the majority of *Behold His Glory* came to birth at 4:30 a.m.

Of course, come night and I drop out from the human race. For me, committees that stretch beyond 9:00 p.m. are a torture and an abomination, and by 11:00 p.m. I'm the quintessential party pooper.

Over the years I have accumulated a series of alarm clocks. When I left chemistry to study for the ministry, the lab staff gave me a farewell and presented me with the standby for farewells—an alarm clock. That's how I've come by all my alarm clocks—someone gave them to me.

Here's the joke: alarm clocks never work for me. If I

have to make an early-morning flight and I set the alarm for 4:00 a.m. or whatever, something funny begins to happen inside my morning morning body. I'm always awake *before* 4:00 a.m. In fact, I wake up first about 2:00 a.m., look at the clock, and go back to sleep. About an hour later another signal goes off inside my head, and I check the time again. By 3:45, I've made three or four checks, so I shut off the alarm and get up.

When we lived at Spicer College in India, sometimes I took students on excursions that left in the dead of night. But we had a fail-safe system in a Nepalese student named Bajaram.

Bajaram had a water alarm clock. He had fine-tuned it, and it never missed. It ran on water, following a formula carefully calculated from years of experience. If Bajaram wanted to wake up at 5:00, before retiring he'd drink two glasses of water; for 4:30, three glasses; for 4:00, four glasses; and so on.

He had the cleanest kidneys on campus.

I wonder: Do marriage counselors realize what a factor for compatibility or chaos we have going here? Do they ever ask couples contemplating marriage what time they like to go to bed and get up?

Think what happens if a morning morning person marries a night night one. They will hardly ever see each other, and never when each is at the peak. One enjoys the twilight's first dawning, the other moonlight. Except that there may not be any roses to go with it.

So definitely, add the morning/night factor to your 24PF and other tests.

And I wonder: What will that celestial morning be like? If I should go the way of all flesh and sleep the long sleep with Adam, what divine alarm will ring through my dust, stirring my members, getting me on my feet to greet the new day?

Will I waken to the sound of music?

Yes, a trumpet blast.

And, I suspect, a roll of drums and the voices of 10 zillion angels in festal chorus.

And a voice. His voice.

Calling. Calling me. Calling me home.

I shall spring from the earth and run to greet Him. I shall fly through the air and embrace Him.

And—sorry, you night people—it will be morning.

Morning forever.

There "we shall ever feel the freshness of the morning and shall ever be far from its close."

CHAPTER 19

Osho

Back in Pune, India, and the newspaper headline reads: "Disciples Flocking Commune for Osho's Birthday."

Osho? Recall him as Rajneesh, he of the long beard, headpiece, and 97 Rolls-Royces. And when *60 Minutes* asked why the guru needed 97 Rolls-Royces, his chief assistant answered, "Why not?"

Why not, indeed?

So Rajneesh used to cruise around Rajneeshpuram, the town he had created in Oregon, near Antelope. His followers came from all over North America, from Europe, from Australia and New Zealand. They put on maroon robes, meditated, hugged, danced, copulated.

Rajneesh had introduced a new path to enlightenment—sex. A lot of people thought it sure beat pilgrimages.

Eventually the whole shebang collapsed. Rumors of assassination attempts. Charges laid by United States marshals. Guruji jetted off in the middle of the night, leaving his fleet of Rolls-Royces behind. But when the plane made a stop for fuel, the marshals were waiting. They expelled him from the United States.

So off to Pune went Rajneesh.

That was where he had started, back in the 1970s. Just before we left India, he had set up an ashram. You could pay your money and sit at his feet as he lectured.

We never did.

We were amazed when a few years later he moved to the United States. Amazed that so many people would flock to him.

Rajneesh's return to India didn't kill his movement, the shady circumstances of his departure from the States notwithstanding. If anything, it grew faster.

And he changed his name. To Osho.

He died in 1990, age 58.

Again, rumors of intrigue. Poisoned by the CIA. Thallium, said his followers. Surrounded by a close-knit circle of advisers. No public appearance for weeks. Then suddenly, his death announced, and instantly cremated. Some reporters speculate: AIDS.

Does the Osho/Rajneesh deal wind up? Not on your life. Osho meditation centers multiply in the year following his death—700 outside India, 250 in India. And now, on the first birthday after his death, 10,000 followers stream into Pune.

Death? No, say his followers.

Osho was never born. He never died. He just passed through.

With a friend I go out to see what's happening.

Before we even reach Osho's center, the streets are jammed—auto rickshaws, vendors selling long maroon robes, eating places, some catering to Western tastes.

Osho is good for business.

Near the center, many foreigners in maroon robes. Young.

Almost all White. One or two Blacks. A couple Indians.

They clasp one another. Hug. Laugh. Kiss.

Men and women. Women and women. Men and men.

We go up to the gate. No, we may not enter, but go next door and we'll find a guide who will show us around.

In the reception area they're signing up young people with packs on their backs.

A tall man with a long white beard and maroon robe, maybe 55, spots us, sizes us up. "Hi, I'm Sam. I'll be with you in a moment."

He's orienting a woman with a heavy German accent. She looks uncertain. She fills out forms.

My friend snaps a photograph. Sam rushes over. "No pictures!" His eyes burn. He points to a sign on the wall.

The woman gets her ID. Sam hugs her. "This is your official welcome," he tells her.

Now he takes us through the gate, and we start the tour. Along the way he tells us about himself: military officer, CIA, professor of business in a Kentucky university. He's been coming to the center for 13 years. One stint lasted three years.

We come to Buddha Hall. It's the largest "hall" enclosed by mosquito netting in the world, Sam tells us. Nothing is happening there at this noonday hour, but a bulletin board announces activities—dances, meditations—for the day.

In another building people are signing up for courses. Sam tells us about one that he took: for the first week three hours every day laughing, the next week three hours crying, the third week three hours of silence every day.

Farther along, a line of people wait to enter Osho's dwelling. Followers only. We can't get in.

A store: books, video tapes, audiocassettes. Everything with Osho's words—speeches transcribed, videotaped.

That's it: tour over. We have the feeling we haven't seen everything. We've had the tour, not seen the center.

Back in the reception area, Sam puts on a video for us and turns to help more new arrivals. The video sets out Osho's manifesto—a new humanity as the world's only hope.

The video starts out with Adventist end-time footage. Wars. Starving children. Environment in peril. The world going to pot. The failure of all human efforts.

Then it gives Osho's solution: the new humanity.

How? Through meditation.

The video's message sends a chill up my spine. Eerie echoes here of the Adventist message. But ultimately, a fundamentally different idea of what the new humanity will be like. And how it becomes new.

That night, nights after, I am haunted.

Faces. Young faces. White faces. Faces laughing. Faces smiling.

But a strange look in their eyes.

And the laughter—something strange. Phony. Maybe the way you laugh after you've spent three hours a day for a week learning how to laugh?

Faces.

Frightening faces. Laughing, but not attractive.

My heart aches for these young people.

They have crossed the oceans, spent their money, followed a dream.

I think they found a nightmare. Will they wake up?

And another face haunts me.

Long white beard. Headpiece. Unblinking. Slow speech. Not attractive, but mesmerizing. Osho.

And then—another face.

He drove no Rolls-Royce—He walked. Once He rode a donkey. No adulation for Him. No thousands of followers. Only three Wise Men came from afar, bringing gifts at His birth.

Ninety-seven Rolls-Royces—why not? "For even the Son of Man did not come to be served, but to serve, and to give his life as a ransom for many" (Mark 10:45, NIV).

He preached a new humanity long before Osho. "I tell you the truth, no one can see the kingdom of God unless he is born again" (John 3:3, NIV). "Therefore, if anyone is in Christ, he is a new creation; the old has gone, the new has come!" (2 Cor. 5:17, NIV).

That—*He*—is the way to the new world order. To peace.

In Jesus. Only Jesus.

You don't have to go to Pune to find Him.

Or to Mecca.

Or to Jerusalem.

He is only a heart-cry away.

CHAPTER 20

Getting In

Getting in is the hard part. Past the flunkies basking in the reflected glory of the Great One and reveling in the little authority at their command.

The Great One is easy. The Great One puts you at ease, makes you feel important, shows an interest in you.

But getting in—running the gauntlet of little people trying to show you how big they are, wallowing in office and officiousness—can try your patience. As we found to our chagrin at the American embassy in Bombay.

We had been called from our work in India to teach at the SDA Theological Seminary at Andrews University. We had the call, and we had letters from the president of Andrews University and the secretary of the General Conference recommending us to the embassy authorities.

But the little man in Bombay gave us a hard time. Why, I don't know to this day. Maybe because we were on our way to the United States, and he would have liked to be in our shoes. More likely, because he had a little authority. He was the keeper of the door—he controlled the way in, processing visa applications—and he wanted to flaunt it.

So he kept us waiting for months. We completed all the formalities—police clearances from every place we'd lived, health clearances, tax clearances—but still nothing moved.

Down to Bombay we'd go by taxi every few weeks. Four, five hours of nerve-tingling travel each way. Once, at the start of the descent of the Ghats—the switchback road down the mountains—a truck struck us from behind and folded the little Fiat taxi like a concertina. Noelene and I in the back seat shot up and banged our heads, but crawled out unhurt.

At the embassy, always the same runaround.

"Wait. Not ready yet. No date for your interview. Don't call me, I'll call you."

But he never did.

Time was running out. We had to get to Australia, then on to the United States to be ready for fall classes. We had to make airplane reservations.

An American friend, disgusted at the delay, devised a plan. She had business at the embassy, and she took Noelene along. Right past the flunkies she marched, Noelene in tow, to a desk where an American woman sat. The flunkies assumed both women were U.S. citizens and didn't raise a finger.

Our friend quickly explained the situation. Within days we had an appointment for the visa interview.

On the morning of the interview, the little man saw us in line. "What are you doing here?" he demanded. When he learned we had gone over his head, he threatened and stormed. But we got our interview—and our visas.

I have met many leaders. Several heads of state. Leaders of Christian communions. Industrial magnates.

Invariably I have found them pleasant, cordial, un-hurried. They feel no need to strut. They make the getting in worth the trouble.

At Spicer College I taught large classes. I spent many hours out of class talking with students. During my last couple of years at the seminary I was associate dean and processed all applications plus a mass of other material. Students came by appointment. Pam Swanson, my secretary, coordinated the flow of bodies.

But during those years at Spicer and Andrews, two individuals frequently came to see me without appoint-ment. They would walk in unannounced, often without knocking. Faculty members or students who were with me would look startled at the intrusion.

That was the deal for these individuals, however. No appointment ever needed. No restricted access.

Terry and Julie.

My children knew they could see me anytime they wanted. Sometimes, I think, they came not because they had anything important for me to hear, but simply to enjoy their unlimited access.

Unlimited access! I love that idea.

Once when Jesus was debating with the Jewish leaders, He said: "Now a slave has no permanent place in the family, but a son belongs to it forever" (John 8:35, NIV).

That's the difference: We are God's sons and daughters, not His servants. We don't have certain hours when we have a right to get inside; we *always* belong inside.

The book of Hebrews strongly supports this idea, which is another reason I love it so much. Great as the earthly sanctuary was, the apostle tells us, it restricted access. To get into the holy place, you had to be a Levite; to get into the Most Holy, a son of Aaron, a high priest. And you could get in only once a year, on Yom Kippur.

But we who believe in Jesus have access.

Access to a greater, more perfect sanctuary than the earthly one.

Access to the very throne room of God.

Access every day, every hour.

Access through the blood of Jesus.

No barriers now. No wall of partition.

Access to every son and daughter of Adam—and of Jesus.

No need for an appointment.

No need for Mary or any "saint" to help us get in.

No need to knock.

Come boldly, joyfully.

Come as God's child.

We *belong* in God's presence.

Getting in is easy.

CHAPTER 21

Oz

In Oz again, and two impressions hit me as I step from the plane—how clean the air, how bright the light!

They talk about a pollution problem, but I see no sign of it. The bush glistens. The sky is azure. The stars sparkle in dark velvet.

I had forgotten how beautiful the Australian bush is. Maybe I hadn't ever looked at it on its own terms before.

That's something that has changed: the way Ozzies look at the land. When I grew up here, the attitude was love-hate, with the latter predominating. Today love has won out.

The first Australians all came from England, Scotland, and Ireland. Many of them had free passage, courtesy of His Majesty's government—clapped in irons in the bowels of transportation ships. For some 80 years after her founding in 1788, Oz was a dumping ground for England's petty thieves and embezzlers and for political troublemakers from Ireland. An antipodean gulag necessitated by the cutting off of the American gulag following revolt of the 13 Atlantic Seaboard colonies.

Those men and women sent here in chains, and the many free settlers who came seeking a better life, found themselves in an alien land, starkly different from the green fields and woods they had left behind.

For the first century of settlement, Oz poets and writers, such as they were, wrote about Oz in the language of England. They were way down south, but their hearts and words had stayed behind.

They found little to praise in this harsh, dry land stretching vastly into only God knew what sort of interior. This land of naked Blacks, too primitive to grow crops or stay in one place; this land of animals that jumped across the wilds or glided from trees; this land of endless eucalyptus. They were exiles, far from home.

They wrote of the brooding silence of the Australian bush. Some silence! Kookaburras laughing their heads off, magpies chortling, galahs shrieking, whipbirds cracking. And bellbirds—crystalline, silver, pure, tinkling from afar.

The bush is silent only to English ears.

When I grew up here, Ozzies were beginning to see the bush in new light. A sea change was taking place, but none of us knew it then.

Now the change has come full measure. Ozzies plant native trees and bushes in their gardens instead of English ones. They're jealous to preserve and protect the bush. England is far away, long forgotten, and unlamented.

We used to keep Christmas in good old English style. Huge, hot dinner. Plum pudding.

Outside it might be 100 degrees in the shade.

"Jingle Bells" and "White Christmas" seemed just a

bit ludicrous. As did Santa, sweating his head off in traditional robes.

This year in Oz, my sister served us a meal of salads for Christmas dinner. Nothing hot, not one thing.

And the Oz Christmas cards show Santa in shorts, sitting under an umbrella by the beach, sipping a cold drink. Or with kangaroos pulling his sleigh.

On the radio a children's choir sings a new carol—"Christmas in Australia." It talks about going to church, then to the beach or to the hills for a picnic on December 25.

Americans and Australians also have a love-hate relationship. We fought side by side to turn the tide of the war in the Pacific. And we fought in all-out brawls in the streets of Brisbane during those same years.

Ozzies admire Americans: their smart dress, their smart ideas, their can-do philosophy, their vast land of breathtaking beauty and unparalleled resources.

They don't like the smart-aleck, condescending way "Yanks" often come across. Still unsure about the role of education, Ozzies feel a wee bit threatened by Americans' learning.

And they think that Americans, with all their hard work and achievements, ought to ease up and enjoy life, lighten up and have a good time.

Americans admire Ozzies: their rugged individuality, their frankness, their vast land of harsh beauty that evokes memories of their own frontier times.

They don't understand Ozzies' passion for play, and they find them blunt to the point of rudeness. They'd like to get them working to make Oz into another United States.

But Oz is one land where Americans can come and feel welcomed, where they can drink the water, where people speak the same language (sort of), where the greenback goes a long way.

True, you have to drive on the other side of the road, which scares you out of your pants the first time you do it. And out in the bush you'll see signs warning you to watch out for kangaroos instead of bears.

But in other ways—essential ways—the two lands and the two peoples are very similar. Which means there is plenty of opportunity for respect. And envy.

For Adventists, the ties run closer.

Ellen White came to Australia, built a home here, built up the work here. Along with other pioneer leaders, she laid the foundation for a strong church in Oz.

The health food work grew and prospered here, a model for Adventists everywhere. Products made by Adventists are in every supermarket; ads for them splash on TV.

And this vast land of small population—only 16 million still—has played a role in the world church way beyond its comparatively small Adventist population.

From Avondale College, predicted Ellen White, missionaries would go out not only to the islands of the South Pacific but to Southern Asia and to South America.

And they have.

And some—many—to the church's world headquarters.

Francis D. Nichol was Australian-born.

C. H. Watson, Australian, led the world church through the years of greatest financial crisis, 1930-1936.

E. L. Minchin. Roy Allan Anderson. W. G. Turner. Lance Butler.

And many others.

I was just a boy when World War II raged, but I still remember songs of that era. Ozzies and Yanks, fighting together, side by side, to win.

We're still in a war, we followers of Jesus. A real war.

Ozzies. Yanks.

And Europeans. Hispanics. Asians.

All together.

And by God's grace we're gonna win.

CHAPTER 22

Tomatoes

Robert Frost wrote that good neighbors are made by good fences.

Recently our neighbors took down the chain-link fence on the boundary of our properties. Took it down, and didn't replace it.

They did so with our approval—yea, encouragement. Years before, we'd had a gate put in the chain-link fence, but even that had become too much of a formality.

So old Robert Frost was wrong. When your neighbors are good friends, you can take away the fences.

Bob and Ellen have been our friends for 20 years. It was a piece of rare fortune when we moved to the Washington, D.C., area and looked for a home that we found one that adjoined theirs, back-to-back.

Bob, among other abilities, has the gardener's green touch. His zucchini grows fast enough and big enough to feed the neighborhood. But tomatoes—they're his specialty.

In the depths of winter's blast, Bob is consulting the latest Burpee seed catalog. Before the frost and the bitter north winds have gone, his seedlings are sprouting in the basement.

Come summer, Bob's tomatoes grow tall, prolific, red. Homegrown tomatoes, picked from the vine—they expose the ones on the supermarket shelves for the imitations they are.

Now, I too like to garden. We'd come from Berrien County, Michigan, where the soil is black and deep and you have only to throw seeds in the ground and come back after a couple summer months to haul away the harvest.

Washington isn't Berrien Springs. You toil for every ounce of success you win from the land. The earth is clay—gumbo when it rains, cement when it bakes out. You have to bring in soil—buy it, make it from humus, create a garden.

After you've toiled and sweated and your plants find a home, the invasion begins. Squirrels. Groundhogs. And an army of bugs, beetles, and blight that attack below the ground and above.

Plus—we have *many* trees out back. Tall trees. Close together.

Which means lots of shade.

For years I tried to grow a garden. I wrestled with the ground, bought and brought in soil, dug, hoed, and scraped.

I tried berries.

I tried lettuce.

I tried tomatoes.

But no garden does well in shade. The year outside would start out fine—until the trees leafed out.

The raspberries were as sour as lemons.

The squirrels ate the nectarines.

Bugs bit through the lettuce.

And tomatoes do not—definitely do not—like shade.

One year I got a bright idea. Bob had Burpees; I would have Behnke's.

Behnke's is a fabulous nursery. Their flowers are so exquisite, their plants so healthy, their layout so attractive, I defy anyone to leave empty-handed.

In early April, while Bob's tomatoes were still four-inch plants, I brought home a royal tomato bush. A young tree, in fact—couple feet tall. In a pot.

And with real tomatoes already in place.

I set the pot on the back patio, watered, watched, and waited.

Bob called "Foul!" and conceded the first tomatoes of the season.

I had the first tomatoes. They weren't very large and their flavor wasn't great, but they were mine.

I figured they cost me about $3.00 each.

Bob had the last tomatoes. And all the others in between.

My first tomatoes were also my last tomatoes. Even tomatoes that come into the world at Behnke's don't do well unless they get plenty of sunlight.

Somewhere in this story I feel a moral lurking, but it hasn't come out of hiding yet.

Maybe it's lurking in the shade.

CHAPTER 23

Trace Elements

The first settlers came to South Australia in July 1836. They came ashore on Kangaroo Island, a land mass about 90 miles long and 30 miles wide lying some 10 miles from the mainland.

Far from England's green and pleasant shores, they began to tame the land. They planted mulberry and almond trees, carefully nurtured during the long voyage, and built the first rough dwellings on the island.

One mulberry tree from 1836 still survives. Its spreading branches held up by steel supports, it bears prodigal harvests of sweet berries.

But the little settlement did not thrive. Its water supply was uncertain, and crops refused to grow in the virgin soil won from the bush. The pioneers lost heart and moved to the Oz mainland, leaving a remnant on Kangaroo Island.

On the mainland, the new colony prospered and grew. Boatload after boatload of new settlers swelled its numbers.

But not much changed on Kangaroo Island. Fishing, sealing, eucalyptus oil, gum from the yucca bushes—a small population found a livelihood.

I grew up in South Australia, in Adelaide, its capital, eight miles from the sea. Once or twice the family went to Cape Jervis at the tip of the peninsula, and we looked out across the Southern Ocean and strained to catch a glimpse of Kangaroo Island.

In elementary school we'd learned about our state. We'd studied the history and traced the map.

Over in the southeast part of the state, the map showed a desolate area labeled "Ninety Mile Desert." It received sufficient rainfall for crops, but crops wouldn't grow there. Nor would sheep—they were sickly and suffered from what the locals called "coast disease."

It was still called the Ninety Mile Desert, but the land was changing while we were learning geography.

The desert was beginning to bloom.

Trace elements.

Chemists discovered that adding minute amounts of copper, molybdenum, and cobalt made the soil fertile. It grew crops; sheep thrived.

They added them to the fertilizer—tiny, tiny percentages. Traces.

Which got me to thinking.

Life throws so many surprises at us. Some of our classmates who seemed to have everything going for them—the ones we voted most likely to succeed—never succeeded. And others we passed over, hardly noticed, have outstanding careers.

I wonder: Could trace elements be part of the reason?

Gifted students have a problem: grades come too

easy. They get the grades—for a while—but don't develop discipline.

At rarefied academic or professional levels you need doggedness, courage, optimism, decisiveness, in order to make it.

How many thousands of DWDs (doctors without dissertations) are walking around? They struggled through the coursework, passed their comprehensives, got their proposal accepted, but couldn't quite wrap it all up.

All that effort, all that money spent, but no Ph.D. degree.

Trace elements.

I wonder: How many marriages falter—after 10, 20, 30, yes 40 years—because they lack trace elements?

Little affections. "I love you." A kiss. A hug.

Little acts of thoughtfulness.

Little acts of creativity to keep the relationship fresh and fun.

I wonder: How many careers get derailed because someone showed up late for an interview or a board meeting?

I wonder: How many people who start so well in the Christian way never make it to the finish line because of a want of trace elements?

Hope.

Good humor.

Counting one's blessings.

"Let your conversation be always full of grace, seasoned with salt," says Paul (Col. 4:6, NIV).

Trace elements.

And Kangaroo Island? They found that a speck of copper and a speck of cobalt transformed the soil.

Today 4,500 people live there.

And 1.3 million sheep.

CHAPTER 24

Knowing Best

Who knows best? I'll tell you who doesn't.

Father.

In high school my best subjects were science and math. I found pure pleasure in solving problems that stumped others. At times I worked on math teasers during vacation—for fun.

Alas, neither of our children inherited those genes. They took enough math and chemistry to meet graduation requirements and no more.

So when my son, during his freshman year in college, announced that he was switching to an economics major, I said to myself, *He'll never be able to handle the math.*

And when later he started on a master's program in international business, I knew he'd be in trouble. The advanced math would do him in.

I knew, but I kept silent.

He had to find his own way, discover for himself

where his abilities lay. He had to find out what I already knew.

Turns out I was the one who had more to learn.

I thought I knew his abilities, but I was wrong. In fact, I was *really* dumb. When he graduated with honors for his B.A. degree, I should have wised up that he had way more ability in math than I thought.

He'd had the ability all along, but it didn't show in high school. Mine did. I had a teacher who turned me on to math; he didn't.

Then there's my little girl . . .

During her senior year of college, she came to me and told me she had interviewed for a master's program at Northwestern University. When I congratulated her, she said, "As far back as I can remember I intended to get a graduate degree."

How come I didn't know that?

In the same way I didn't know that my little girl was now a grown woman.

Father doesn't know best.

He only thinks he does.

Maybe Mother does. She treasured up a glory box of sayings and actions from the kids' early years—stuff that passed through and out of my head. Maybe she understands the children, sees them as they are, what they can be.

I wonder.

Maybe it's the kids' fault after all. They make Father think he knows best. For a few years Father is Superman, Joe Montana, and king of the earth. He's a giant and can do anything in the whole wide world. He knows best.

Too soon comes the day of cruel awakenings—for the child.

It comes much later for Father.

By far the hardest part of parenting is letting go.

Letting our kids make their own way.

Letting them get burned.

Letting them succeed.

The more we love them, the harder it seems to let them go.

The more we love them, the more we will want to let them go.

There has been only one perfect Father. His home is perfect, His love unflawed by impatience or anger, His training impeccable in discipline and child psychology.

But He let His children go. Let them make their own way, their own mistakes, their own successes.

Even though He knows best.

CHAPTER 25

Rain Sound

To appreciate rain, you have to live in dry country. And to appreciate the rain sound, you have to live in a house with a "tin" roof.

I grew up in dry country. Southern Australia near the coast gets maybe 20 inches of precipitation a year, but inland the land rarely sees rain. Way out back, in the center—what they used to call the dead heart of Oz—you can meet kids 2, 3 years old who've never seen it rain.

I grew up in a house with a tin roof—galvanized iron. In the summer, when a change would sweep in to break the 100-degree heat, we'd hear the rain coming. Smell it in the air, and hear it approaching across the rooftops.

Recently my brother Doug built a new home in southern Australia. Tin roof. "We want to be able to hear the rain," said his wife.

To this day some of the loveliest music I know comes through the open window as I lie in bed and listen to the rain. Our home in Silver Spring, Maryland, has a shingle roof, so we get our rain jollies from the side instead of from above.

Maryland isn't dry country: 40 inches of rain, sometimes more, every year. And sometimes the heavens pour out a deluge.

Like the monsoon.

Month after month, you wait for the Indian sky to change. You scan the papers to see if the monsoon is on track, working its way up the subcontinent.

The land lies cracked, baked, arid, dead.

The air hangs still, hot, stifling.

Then the clouds roll in. With fire and light, the heavens burst open.

The drops begin. A few. They come, bearing dust.

Then more and more, larger and closer.

You run outside and let the watery life flow over your hair, your face, your hands. Soaking. Cooling. Renewing.

By now the heavens have gone crazy. Inside, outside, all you hear is rain sound—drumming, drumming, drumming.

Once I was conducting a Week of Prayer at the Adventist boarding school in Assam, in the mountains of northern India. In the middle of one of the meetings the rain began—and I stopped.

We tried to sing, but couldn't hear ourselves. Not the piano. Nothing—only the rain.

Once, long ago, the rain came with a fury and a roar that wiped out everything else. The rain took over. There was nothing anyone could do.

"When the day of Pentecost came, they were all together in one place. Suddenly a sound like the blowing of a violent wind came from heaven and filled the whole house where they were sitting. They saw what seemed to be tongues of fire that separated and came to rest on each of them. All of them were filled with the Holy Spirit and began to speak in other tongues as the Spirit enabled them" (Acts 2:1-4, NIV).

We are in dry country.

Even in Silver Spring, Maryland, where we get 40 inches of precipitation each year. And where the General Conference headquarters is located.

I'm waiting for the rain sound.

CHAPTER 26

Chain Saw

Recently I bought a chain saw. And I thereby entered the fraternity.

A maple—tall, spreading, and scraggly—started it all. Planted with the house some 25 years ago, its branches now hung over the roof. In a strong wind it groaned and creaked and swept against the shingles. My wife and I wondered when we'd wake up one dark and stormy night and find the maple in bed with us.

No question: the maple had to go.

I tried trimming the maple. It grew taller and thicker. It put out branches way up where I couldn't get to them. It fled to the roof from me.

The maple had to go.

Enter the tree service people. Yes, they would remove the maple—for $400.

Four hundred dollars! I'd never paid a cent to have a tree cut down. Enter our friends Denise and Alberto. One evening Denise recounted Alberto's chain saw exploits. A recent member of the fraternity, he knocked off every tree in sight after practicing on a dresser given by his friend.

For $400 I could buy a gaggle of chain saws.

I bought one. Electric job. On sale for $69.95.

Now we planned the Great Assault. I warmed up on the apple tree in the backyard. It fell without a whimper. I knocked off the Japanese plum to perfect my handling skills.

Then, to the enemy.

Which was assembled on three fronts. The maple had three large branches. Two reached out over the front lawn. The third, largest and highest, over the roof.

We brought down the first branch with masterful strategy. With Noelene pulling on a rope attached to its limbs, it fell within inches of the designated spot.

The second branch was a bit more tricky. It reached toward the electric wires and our neighbor's carport. I saw him observing us apprehensively.

But again Noelene's rope maneuver did the trick. Enemy defeated on the second front.

Now only one branch remained. But it was high. Very high. Too high to handle from the ground.

And it was big. Very big. And over the roof. The physics of the matter were unassailable, no matter how you figured: the branch would crash onto the roof.

We retired from the battle scene to rethink strategy. For several weeks we had a deformed maple in our front yard—a torso with one huge branch hanging over our roof.

On Labor Day we decided to attack. We would go for broke. We would chain-saw the maple at the base, relying on Noelene's rope wizardry to get us through.

It would be our biggest test by far. We stood to lose:
One roof.

One neighbor's carport.

One neighbor's roof.

Electric supply to the neighborhood.

The maple was surprisingly big at the base. The cut swallowed up our little electric chain saw. I had to come at it from one side, then the other.

We almost had the maple at our mercy. It swayed in the breeze, tottering on a sliver of supporting fiber.

Noelene and I strained on the rope.

The maple teetered and tottered.

Actually, it teetered more than it tottered. Meaning it was going to crash through our roof.

Again, the inexorable laws of physics: the huge branch over the roof made the teeter greater than the totter.

Enter our neighbor Bob. He flung his weight on the rope.

The totter prevailed. The maple crashed to the lawn with a blow that rattled the neighbors' windows.

Fallen giant. It stretched diagonally across the lawn, to the edge of the street.

We set to cutting it up. And had wood for many winter fires.

And stories to share around them. For we quickly discovered that everyone with a chain saw has stories to tell.

I had joined the fraternity. Including the president of the General Conference, we found out beside one fire. An impeccable source told how, when Elder Folkenberg goes off backpacking on his own, as he likes to do from time to time, he takes along his chain saw. He not only cuts wood enough for his own needs but for five years' worth of campers.

Once, males put on chaps and a Stetson, slung

six-shooters to their waists, sauntered to their steeds and with a "Hi-yo, Silver" galloped into the sunset.

Real men.

They died with their boots on.

Today they die with their chain saws by their side.

Real men.

I foresee a national convention—I'm amazed no one has thought of it yet—of chain saw owners. The NCCSO will have chapters in every state. In New York City they can be especially creative.

Think of the crowds at the annual gathering. Hear the announcer's call: "Gentlemen, start your motors!"

They could deforest the state of Washington in one day.

I'm still trying to figure out why I get so much of a kick out of my chain saw. Normally I detest destruction—graffiti, vandalism, smashing—but I love the way the chain blade slices through wood. The ease with which it fells a giant.

Maybe it's the power thing after all. The fascination we feel at raw strength.

And our control of it.

There's something almost godlike here, something akin to the Creator. Maybe a hint, a residue of our being made in His image. Even the ability to destroy. For, as little as some Christians like to contemplate the idea, the Creator is also Destroyer.

Our being made in His image brings that ability also. It is, I guess, the most abused aspect of our humanity in these times.

The ability to destroy is a fearful thing in the hands of fallen men and women. Small wonder that we entertain grave misgivings about execution of criminals.

Or maybe the chain saw is only a toy—a grown man's toy. The boy still hides inside every man. That too is a residue of the divine image.

Nevertheless, remember our fallenness. So, if you ask a grown man of sterling character—steady, dependable, predictable—to bring his chain saw and cut down one of your trees, you'd best keep an eye on him. He'll find several more to remove while he's at it.

CHAPTER 27

The Call

The hardest decision of my life—one that I fought the Lord over for months—wasn't accepting Jesus. It was to leave the work for which I had trained and in which I was employed—industrial chemistry—and prepare for the ministry.

Noelene's sharpest moment of truth came later, when we were students together at Avondale College. Early in our final year there the dean, Dr. Ivan Higgins, called us to his office. An American who had served in India, he was liaison officer for Pacific Union College, with which Avondale was then affiliated.

Higgins loved to reminisce about Southern Asia. This afternoon he fell into a pensive mood, seemed far away. He began to tell us about a school way up in the mountains, up where the clouds form, where you can look out over the plains of India and see for 100 miles, where rhododendrons grow wild over the mountains and bloom in the spring.

On and on he went. We enjoyed his soliloquy but

wondered when he would get to the point.

Higgins paused. He looked us straight in the eye. "A call will be coming for you both," he said. "Southern Asia is looking for a dean of boys and Bible teacher at Vincent Hill School, as well as a piano teacher."

Noelene was taking piano along with elementary education. I was assistant preceptor (men's dean) at Avondale.

But . . .

We had not applied for overseas service.

We weren't married.

We weren't even engaged.

And Noelene's parents. How they would react to this call out of the blue? Noelene's father, an Adventist minister, and mother had taught their children never to refuse a call. We decided, in our naivete, to wait till the official call came to tell them about Higgins' startling conversation.

Problem: the call didn't come.

Month after month went by, and still no call.

Higgins was puzzled. "Have you received the call yet?" he would ask. "I can't understand it. The Southern Asia Division voted it months ago."

The call had come—but not to us. Following denominational protocol it had arrived in Wahroonga, Australasian Division headquarters. There it sat. The "brethren," puzzled and a trifle vexed that Southern Asia planned to pull away two of their graduates who hadn't even asked for mission service, let the leaders in India cool their heels. They decided to release the call to us only at the end of the Avondale school year—November—when the other graduates received their calls to the field.

Meanwhile, a rumor began to circulate on campus.

The students used to have a stock expression, spoken humorously, to one another: "Greetings from Southern Asia." Well, the rumor said that Southern Asia actually planned to call a young man and a young woman from the graduating class.

Noelene's brother heard the rumor. He had seen Noelene and me talking with Higgins, saw how concerned we both had been for months, and put two and two together. He went to Higgins to confirm his suspicions.

The cat was out of the bag.

And we were in deep, deep trouble.

No call. And worse, no letter to Noelene's family.

We tried to explain, but our explanation seemed weak.

India was out of the question. Even though the family prayed for missionaries. Even though Pastor and Mrs. Taylor had held up the ideal of mission service.

Not for their daughter. Their only daughter.

Not India.

They had our future mapped out. I would work a year or two in the ministry, prove I could cut the mustard. Then I might be suitable to marry their daughter.

Others—senior ministers, my home church pastor—warned us about India. Maybe you'll get sick and your health will be broken. You'll get lost over there—come back home and no one will know you, and you won't have a job in the ministry.

On campus the students were happy for us, some envious.

For Noelene, a trial by fire.

I knew what to do. The hard call for me had come three years earlier, when I wrestled with the Lord for

118

months before deciding to quit chemistry. Going to India would be easy after going to Avondale.

For Noelene, weeks of searching.

Searching to know herself. Searching her heart, her love for me.

Searching her relationship to her parents.

Searching to find out God's will for her.

During those days of pain and tears, these words from Ellen White brought comfort and guidance to both of us: "The Lord will teach us our duty just as willingly as He will teach somebody else. If we come to Him in faith, He will speak His mysteries to us personally. Our hearts will often burn within us as One draws nigh to commune with us as He did with Enoch. Those who decide to do nothing in any line that will displease God, will know, after presenting their case before Him, just what course to pursue. And they will receive not only wisdom, but strength" (*The Desire of Ages*, p. 668).

God promised to show us what to do. But to *us*, those directly involved.

Noelene made her decision.

I had made mine weeks before.

If the call came, we would accept it.

On September 1 we received a letter from division headquarters in Sydney. I opened it and immediately realized someone had goofed. The envelope was addressed to me, but the letter was intended for Dr. Gordon McDowell, principal of Avondale College. And it enclosed our official letter of call, to be given us weeks later.

That day Noelene and I announced our engagement.

It was the first day of spring in Australia.

The following months jetted past. Graduation mid-November. Marriage December 21.

January 10—we sailed for India.

We saw Australia, and our parents, again after five and a half years.

I cannot tell you how God leads. I cannot explain why He dealt with Noelene and me as He did. I cannot comprehend the depths and richness of His guidance for us.

But this I believe: God has led, and He still leads us.

And to all who seek to know His will for them—not for others, for them—He will make it known.

In His own time.

In His own way.

CHAPTER 28

Grace

I find it hard to contemplate getting old. I've always been "young Bill" or "Billie" to my brothers and sisters. Everyone else would age, but not I.

And now, with a suddenness that startles me, I have to face my mortality. I may not live forever. I may grow old like the others.

Bill is gone. He for whom I was named; he who taught me cricket, who always took interest in me—my brother-in-law Bill is gone. Alive when I began this book only months ago. Gone.

And Noelene and I have been learning firsthand about nursing homes. Her father now lives in one. His is a good one, but it isn't a place we find attractive. I don't like its smell, its cries that echo into Dad's room, its sights of collapsing bodies and collapsed minds.

A woman walks by slowly. She moves gracefully, a lady. She peers at me intently, fiercely. She doesn't smile, doesn't speak. In her arms she clutches a large doll.

Across the hall from Dad's room—we see him through the open door—a gaunt figure struggles to read the newspaper, his left side fallen, his head at right angles to his body.

Once he stood tall, straight. Once the doll woman smiled and spoke.

Once they were like I now am.

And I—I may be as they are now.

That possibility troubles me. But whatever lies ahead—whether Jesus will come back before I grow old, or I am struck down while I still have strength, or I join the community of the nursing home—I know all will be well.

Grace.

Charlie Lee Brooks, sweet singer of the Adventist family and my friend, fought cancer for years. Fought with a smile, without a complaint.

During his last months he couldn't walk anymore. He'd come to the General Conference headquarters in Silver Spring in a wheelchair, and Gladys would push him around the offices.

One morning I spoke for the General Conference worship, and I saw Charlie Lee at the back, sitting in his wheelchair, eyes shining.

After a while Gladys brought him by the office. "I knew you were going to speak, Bill," he said, "and I wanted to hear it. I knew you would speak about grace."

It was the last time I saw Charlie Lee alive.

At the end of the road that's all we have, all we can cling to.

Grace.

If we knew it, that's all we have now.

" 'Tis grace hath brought me safe thus far,
    And grace will lead me home."

"It is well, it is well with my soul."

If my life should end right now, I would die a happy man. When the Lord gives a blessing, He adds no bitterness to it. Grace upon grace, delight upon delight, pleasures new every morn from the hand of my bountiful God—this has been my life.

Working on this book has been fun, and more. It has reminded me of God's good hand upon me, of His leading, of His tender regard in things large and small.

Of grace.

For grace, as Ellen White said, surrounds us like the air we breathe. We are *in* grace, from the moment of our first breath.

Life, the universe, comes to us. Despite the dark side of human existence, life is *for* us, not against us. New every morning is the Saviour's love. His compassions fail not. Great is His faithfulness.

We are in grace.

I think we cannot define grace, cannot comprehend grace. Grace is divine, not human.

But we can accept grace, rejoice in it. We can breathe the atmosphere and go on our way rejoicing.

As in writing this book. When I began I jotted down a list of possible topics. Now at the close I look over them and notice which ones came to birth. Some topics high on the list—how I came to leave chemistry for the ministry, the world's greatest birthday party, grandchildren, cats, fireworks—didn't get a chance. Others, not contemplated at first, edged them out.

Ah, well, maybe another time . . .

A list. But there can be no list. No list adequate for God's activity.

No list of life.

Only slivers of experience. Snapshots. Images.

No list of grace.
No list of God's goodness in things large and small.
No list of the atmosphere.
Knowing that, I reckon, is the most important wising up of all.

Also by William Johnsson

Behold His Glory
This devotional book brings new and clearer insights into Christ's birth, boyhood, ministry, death, and resurrection. Hardcover, 400 pages. US$9.95, Cdn$12.45.

Blessed Assurance
Dr. Johnsson takes an intriguing look at Habakkuk and Hebrews and presents their common theme of full assurance. Paper, 144 pages. US$6.95, Cdn$8.70.

I Chose Adventism
William and Noelene Johnsson help us relate to family, friends, and business associates who haven't chosen our Adventist lifestyle. Paper, 128 pages. US$7.50, Cdn$9.40.

In Absolute Confidence
Dr. Johnsson helps us to understand the book of Hebrews better and points out its significance for Christians today. Paper, 160 pages. US$8.95, Cdn$11.20.

Why I Am a Seventh-day Adventist
This booklet explains why the Seventh-day Adventist Church appeals to so many people. It's great for sharing with those who have questions about our faith. Paper, 32 pages. US$.79, Cdn$1.00.

The Wit and Wisdom of Charles Bradford
This is Bradford speaking from the pulpit, in high-level councils, and in private conversation. You hear his most eloquent speeches, his most entertaining anecdotes. Compiled by William and Noelene Johnsson. Paper, 136 pages, plus two 60-minute audiocassettes. US$9.95, Cdn$12.45.

To order, call **1-800-765-6955** or write to ABC Mailing Service, P.O. Box 1119, Hagerstown, MD 21741. Send check or money order. Enclose applicable sales tax and 15 percent (minimum US$2.50) for postage and handling. Prices and availability subject to change without notice. Add 7 percent GST in Canada.

Inspirational Reading

But God, I'm So Humble Already
Aletha Pineda redeems humility from its doormat connotation
and recognizes it as a valuable trait for getting along with others.
True stories show how exercising humility averts personal
conflict, builds self-confidence, and even triggers a sense of
humor. Paper, 96 pages. US$6.95, Cdn$8.70.

Gospel in the Grocery Store
These lighthearted parables spring from Kay Rizzo's trips to the
supermarket—the unruly shopping cart, the impersonal mob,
generic products in their insignificant wrappers—and reveal
eye-opening truths about ourselves, God, and the people in our
lives. Paper, 95 pages. US$4.95, Cdn$6.20.

In Pastures Green
In 1975 Bev Condy left the rush of city life and took up farming
in the Sierra Nevada foothills. Her stubborn, silly sheep, along
with horses, cats, geese, goats, a stray dog, and friendly
neighbors, gave her insights into human nature and God's love.
Paper, 96 pages. US$6.95, Cdn$8.70.

Heaven
David Smith turns our focus from this troubled world and helps
us imagine what it will be like to live in heaven with Jesus
forever. Paper, 96 pages. US$7.95, Cdn$9.95.

To order, call **1-800-765-6955** or write to ABC Mailing Service, P.O. Box
1119, Hagerstown, MD 21741. Send check or money order. Enclose
applicable sales tax and 15 percent (minimum US$2.50) for postage and
handling. Prices and availability subject to change without notice. Add 7
percent GST in Canada.

WHAT HAS GOD DONE FOR US LATELY?

Remember the way the Lord has led us in our past history. And if you want something more current, subscribe to the *Adventist Review*, and see what God did for us last week.

You'll read wonderful stories about doors opening in countries where we once faced a brick wall. You'll hear about big baptisms. And you'll share in the inspiring experiences of other Adventists.

Subscribe to the weekly *Adventist Review*, and see what God has done for us lately.

Blessings reported as they happen. In the weekly

ADVENTIST REVIEW

To order, call your local Adventist Book Center:

1-800-765-6955